STILL
LIVING
STILL

Walking in Peace During Life's Trials

By

Abby Lewis

STILL LIVING STILL
Walking in Peace During Life's Trials

© 2022 Abby Lewis

Published by Book Breakthrough Publishing

Scripture quotations taken from the Amplified® Bible (AMP), Copyright © 2015 by The Lockman Foundation. Used by permission. www.lockman.org

Scripture quotations taken from the Amplified® Bible (AMPC), Copyright © 1954, 1958, 1962, 1964, 1965, 1987 by The Lockman Foundation. Used by permission. www.lockman.org

Scripture quotations marked (ESV) are from The ESV® Bible (The Holy Bible, English Standard Version®), copyright © 2001 by Crossway, a publishing ministry of Good News Publishers. Used by permission. All rights reserved.

Scripture quotations marked (NIV) are taken from the Holy Bible, New International Version®, NIV®. Copyright © 1973, 1978, 1984, 2011 by Biblica, Inc. TM Used by permission of Zondervan. All rights reserved worldwide. www.zondervan.com The "NIV" and "New International Version" are trademarks registered in the United States Patent and Trademark Office by Biblica, Inc. TM

Scripture quotations marked (NKJV) are taken from the New King James Version®. Copyright © 1982 by Thomas Nelson. Used by permission. All rights reserved.

Definitions for the words 'still' and 'strife' taken from The New Oxford American Dictionary ('strife' pg 90, 'still' pg 7). McKean, Erin. The New Oxford American Dictionary. New York, N.Y: Oxford University Press, 2005.

Editor: Joy Bollinger, Say It With Joy

ISBN Number: 979-8-218-06944-5

A SPECIAL
NOTE TO MY READERS

There was a time when I struggled to stand strong and courageous during trials. But God has done a deep work in my heart to get me to a place of stability and steadiness in my faith and trust in Him. The purpose of *Still Living Still~Walking in Peace During Life's Trials* is to share the details and authenticity of that deep work.

There may be times when you find my journey difficult to read, because my story might mirror what is in your heart, along with things that God wants to accomplish within you. However, I encourage taking a break if needed, but please don't resist embracing what God may be revealing through my journey.

It is my hope that you read the entire book to grasp how deep God's love is for you. I believe that my life demonstrates God's profound and immeasurable love for all people. He is available to walk together with you and to faithfully carry you through every trial.

God's love has always comforted and encouraged me. It is my prayer that you will experience that comfort and encouragement as I show you how His peace is the foundation and stabilizer of your faith in the midst of trials (2 Corinthians 1:4).

Still Living Still~Walking in Peace During Life's Trials is a continuation of my journey of being raw, real, transparent, and vulnerable. I hope that this book will show you a different way to live. It is my prayer that you will be able to walk victoriously through this world with a peace that surpasses all understanding. It is my hope that you connect with my story and discover that you don't have to be completely uprooted when trials come your way. I want your roots to grow deep as you press into God and persevere during trials and suffering.

ACKNOWLEDGMENTS

A special thanks to my very dear friends, Matt and Becca Ranker, founders of We Shall See. I could not have made this journey without them. Over the years, despite many miles separating us, they have faithfully walked with me through my entire journey, loved me, prayed for me, laughed, and cried with me, spoken life into me, cheered me on, supported me, and helped me to stay strong. They are a true gift from God, and I treasure our beautiful friendship and deeply appreciate and love them.

Matt and Becca Ranker, founders of We Shall See

The Rankers are a family of seven who follow the call of God. He has taken them from almost one end of the country to the other and back again. Their hearts' desire is to meet people wherever they are in life and show them the love of Jesus.

A portion of all profits from the sales *of Still Living Still~Walking in Peace During Life's Trials* will go to support We Shall See.

Follow their journey at www.weshallseeministries.com

FOREWORD

I remember first meeting Abby Lewis sixteen years ago and being struck by her capacity to meet people where they are and to love people deeply, particularly people who are struggling. Our beautiful tourist community of Branson, Missouri, had just started a Loaves & Fishes program during the off-season for local folks who were unemployed, either temporarily or permanently, or who were just seeking fellowship and a warm meal.

I recall that Abby called me with an idea about picking up "guests" from the area long-term rental motels—makeshift homes for those barely getting by—to take them to the designated Loaves & Fishes location. She had convinced the local YMCA to loan her their bus for this purpose. She called the bus "Hope on the Road." Abby's served as the "hostess" of the bus by inviting those in need to climb on board and come for dinner.

Abby's passion for those who are struggling was evident, and her joyful smile and warmth were a powerful magnet to those who timidly walked toward the bus. Who could resist the smile and accepting posture she demonstrated to every single person? Pretty soon, she was referring to the group as family.

Abby learned that the need for love and acceptance is a hunger all people have deep inside, especially those who feel they are on the fringe or different in some way. Loaves & Fishes served as a convening place of love and acceptance. I recall one guest saying, "I feel more loved here than I do with my own family." Abby was an essential part of their experience.

The passion that runs so deep in Abby Lewis spilled out in her first book, *Living Still*, where her transparency concerning her own journey revealed a picture of fear and anxiety and brokenness. The techniques and stories shared in the book resonated with her readers and provided valuable tools for their emotional and relational "toolbox." I found its message "countercultural" in the value that was placed on getting "really still," which is much easier said than done!

In *Still Living Still*, Abby shares the challenges her beautiful son, Shia, faces from autism. These challenges have strengthened Abby's faith in God by giving her the opportunity to put this faith into practice. I am confident that the stillness Abby learned to practice has been a vital tool in her love and care for Shia. Shia lives his best life in a calm and still environment. He thrives in nature, and the peace he discovers there is a beautiful illustration of the way God's creation can minister to each of us, but only if we are still and allow the sun and the wind and the sounds to envelope our bodies.

Over the years, I have heard many, many people of faith say, "Let go and let God." There is no one I know who works more diligently, who sees more clearly, or who listens more earnestly to God's still, small voice than Abby Lewis. God's handiwork is all around us, and we rarely pause long enough to see it, much less enjoy it. The following pages are a primer on how it is done.

Flip on the news at any time of day or night, and you will see and hear the chaos on your screen. This terrifying world of crime, threats, wars, and riots can leave you anxious and discouraged. *Still Living Still* is the antidote to the roar of chaos and confusion all around you. Abby gathered the tools and recognized the benefits of being still long before Shia came into the world. This new work shows what it looks like to be still in the midst of challenges and demonstrates the blessings and peace that result from choosing to live life differently. "Living still" makes all the difference, and readers will benefit from the simple principles and practices contained in these pages.

The world would say that a nonverbal child like Shia has nothing to contribute, but I would argue that Shia's life speaks volume about the rich life God desires for each of us.

Read on, friend, read on.

Sue R. Head, Ed.D.
Vice President for Cultural Affairs &
Dean of Character Education
College of the Ozarks
Point Lookout, Missouri

TABLE OF CONTENTS

A PROPHETIC WORD
SPOKEN IN 2007

It was the summer of 2007. I was being prayed for by a gentleman whom I had just met. During the prayer, he began to have a vision. He said, "I see you speaking. The crowd is small. Wait, it is growing. It is getting bigger and bigger. Wow!! It is like the size of a Woodstock crowd." He then stopped, looked at me in complete surprise and asked, "What are you going to do—write a book?" Although I was excited about this message, I had never written a book, nor had I spoken to a large crowd, so I was somewhat terrified with the thought of it all.

About a month later, I got a call from this same person who had prayed over me. He told me, he was driving and began to have a vision. He said the vision was so powerful, that he had to pull onto the side of the road. He went on to share, "God is going to use you to set the world on fire, Abby." He continued, "I saw this map, and it had pockets of fires here and there. The fires grew and grew until it spread like wildfire across the world."

His words penetrated deep within my soul as he was sharing. Not knowing how or when this would take place, I believed in that moment and with everything in me, that it would happen in God's timing. Little did I know that God would lead me to write the first book, *LIVING STILL~Walking in Peace in the Midst of Life*, which was published in 2011 and then re-released in 2012. Now you are reading my recent release. Only God knows what more He has for me to accomplish.

Chapter 1

GOD'S NUDGINGS
TO WRITE THIS BOOK

Rapid Deployment

My husband, Tim, who is active military, came home from work with some news. With a serious tone, he said, "We need to talk."

We sat at the kitchen table as he proceeded to ask if I had seen the news. I had not. He then explained the circumstances and told me that there was the likelihood that he would rapidly be deploying to help evacuate Americans from a certain country. I responded, "That's interesting, because before I awoke this morning, I had a dream about you leaving suddenly to help people who might be in danger."

It was comforting to know that God had prepared my heart to hear this news. Although it wasn't definite that Tim would be going, he was told by his commander to prepare and be on call for a likely deployment. Without any details involving his potential departure, we were in the dark concerning when he would leave, his return, if we could communicate with one another, and how much danger he would face. This was the first type of rapid deployment in our military career.

I felt uneasy, but I wasn't swayed. I was steady, stable, and firmly planted in God. That night I prayed, "Lord, I trust You. I trust You if he stays. I trust You if he goes." What came out of my mouth next was truly unbelievable and stopped me in my tracks, "I trust You if he dies."

Everything that I had learned over the years, I was able to put into practice at that very moment of my prayer. Freedom is the only word I know to describe what I felt when I spoke those words aloud. I continue to be in awe of the deep work that God has done in my heart.

The next day, the therapist who works with our son, Shia, said she might be leaving at the end of the month due to some circumstances beyond her control. She had worked beautifully with Shia and had been his therapist for about three years and was in our home five days a week for close to two years. We all loved her and had thought of her as an important part of our family. Not wanting to lose her, I felt peace drain from me. Despite the news, I told God, "I trust You. If she must leave, I trust that You have a plan for Shia."

Within a few days, Tim was given the command that they were officially going, yet there was no definite timeline. As a result, Tim was pulled from his half-completed four-week course that was required for a promotion to the next rank. Instead of finishing the necessary training, he would spend his time preparing for deployment.

This possible deployment was a gut punch to both of us, because the four-week course was not an easy course to get into, and it wasn't always available. However, it was out of our control. Instead of focusing on the frustration of our circumstances, we both chose to remain steady and stable as we shifted our focus and began packing for his unpredictable deployment.

Later that night, while I was in the shower, my mind filled with very loud thoughts like, *One day soon, you will be in this shower, sobbing, with your face on that bench, because Tim will be dead.* Although those thoughts were trying to sway me into losing my peace, I was able to stand steady on my faith and say, "I trust You, God."

We were given the official timeline to deploy in a couple of days. Not even a day later, we were told to stand by and relax over the weekend, because they weren't leaving just yet and might not be leaving. They would inform us as they knew any updated information.

The next few days, things were quiet, so we began to think that he would not be leaving. But then the official word came, "We are deploying. Get ready." Then came another pause.

The back-and-forth orders made the situation a bit unsettling. Is he going? Is he staying? We had a few frustrating moments but that was what they were—just moments. We were steady and firmly fixed in our faith, despite all the back and forth and all the hurry up and wait. We couldn't control the circumstances, but we could control our responses. A few more days passed. The deployment was set and final. Tim deployed.

There were many unknowns when we said goodbye to each other. We didn't know when he would return. We had no idea if we would be able to communicate. We weren't sure exactly where he was going or what kind of danger he would face. However, what was beautiful and powerful was the peace that we both had, knowing that we were exactly where we were supposed to be, doing what God was calling us to do, and trusting Him deeply.

Surprisingly, on the very day that Tim told me we needed to talk, I had earlier felt a prompting from God to write this book, which had been stirring within my heart for a time. So, I began the process of journaling all that was going on with Tim's deployment. I felt as though I was being given a final exam on all that God had taught me over the last eleven years.

I stood firm and steady with peace and in complete awe of all that God had brought me through. I could say that I was at a place of stability in my heart with a deeply rooted, unshakable faith, living and walking in peace during life's trials.

God's Message: Don't Quit

On the way home from getting groceries, the license plate on the car in front of me stood out. It seemed like God was saying, "Look at this." It read DONTQUIT. And the car next to it was highlighted with the same intensity. God seemed to be saying, "Look at this one as well." As I glanced over, the number 222 caught my attention. I found it very interesting and only something God could have orchestrated.

I officially started writing *Still Living Still~Walking in Peace During Life's Trials* in February of 2022 (222). God was sending a message with both license plates, "Despite all that you are up against, I need you to remember all I have taught you. Persevere in this. Don't quit."

A Decision to Make

I sat in my rocking chair, staring at our family picture that was hanging on the wall and praying for God's protection over Tim. Our son was snuggled in bed. The house was quiet and still, when unexpectedly, my peace was interrupted by very loud and intrusive thoughts that filled my mind. "Tim will never be coming home. You will be getting a call that he died. You will be a widow." Again, I was able to feel the intensity of those thoughts, but I stood firm and refused to be swayed by the noise in my mind. I remained firmly fixed in God through it all.

That same night, I was in our kitchen getting ready to plug in some things to be charged overnight. When I opened the drawer to get the charger, a box of matches stood out with the words, "You DECIDE." I had opened this drawer every night and had never noticed those words on the box of matches. I immediately heard God speak to my heart, "That's right Abby. You decide what you are going to think about. You decide if you're going to be swayed by those thoughts. You decide if you are going to press into Me for everything you need to walk in peace during this trial."

5

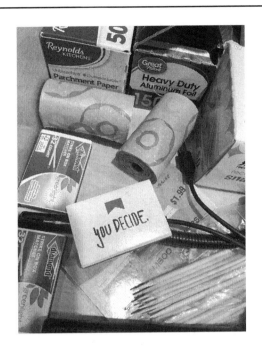

Chapter 2

LIVING STILL IS MY FOUNDATION

L *iving Still* is the foundation I stand on. It was and continues to be the training I rely on so I can continue to walk in peace through all the trials of life. So, what is living still? The *New Oxford American Dictionary* defines "still" as quiet, silent, calm, peaceful, serene, stillness. The scripture tells us to "Be still and know that I am God" (Psalm 46:10 NIV).

Living still is not adopting a life of inactivity or solitude. Living still is choosing to live in tune with the voice of God in the midst of the inevitable noise around us. Living still is recognizing that without God, we cannot experience the fullness of life. It is choosing to trust God more than we trust ourselves and what we see.

Living still is learning to rest in God's perfect love. It is taking the time to listen to His still, small voice with the expectation that He will lovingly guide us, one step at a time, towards freedom. The practice of living still works. Learning to live this way delivered me from the pit after I hit rock bottom in 2002. This way of living continues to transform my life each day. I'm confident that living still can also change your life.

The trials I have endured in the years since the release of my first book are what I share in this book. The intensity of the trials required me to rely on all my training to be still before God as He exposed deeper issues in my heart that needed to be corrected. They had to be exposed and addressed so I could be more of a reflection of who God is, which is what I deeply desire.

A person really doesn't know what is going on in their heart until the intensity of a trial comes into their life. Just as silver is refined in the fire and the impurities rise to the surface to be skimmed off, I too had some impurities come to the surface during my trials that God wanted to skim off.

Anyone can have peace, patience, joy, and self-control when everything is going their way. However, the truest test of a person's character and what God is more concerned about, is how we respond when things are not as we would want them. We must learn how to trust God and pursue peace.

Pursue Peace

A teacher once said, "Where you have no peace, you have no power." God's Word instructs us to "seek peace and pursue it" (Psalm 34:14). When I think of those times when peace was absent, I felt so weakened, that I literally ran in pursuit of God's peace. I have found that when peace is gone, I must do whatever is necessary to restore and maintain it.

My deep desire is to truly walk in peace throughout life and in all its trials. This is something that cannot be done in my own strength. If I don't have peace, that generally means I have a tight grip on a deep-rooted issue in my heart that God wants me to release.

As I went through these intense trials, the fire grew hotter as things were exposed within my heart. As I became uncomfortable, I grabbed even tighter to what I believed might be lost. Immediately the worries and cares of this world would overwhelm and choke the peace out of me.

Going through these trials taught me to keep a tight grip on God and a loose grip on everything else. Now, when peace leaves, even for a moment, I ask myself, "What have I picked up." If need be, I ask the harder questions like: "Why do I keep picking this problem back up? Why does this problem keep surfacing? What is the root issue of my suffering?"

Don't Waste Your Suffering

During my trials, I heard a pastor say, "Don't waste your suffering. Learn from it. Embrace it." That was never my first response to suffering. At first, my natural response was to somehow avoid it. Deeply trusting God can be extremely challenging when the pain seems more than we can endure. But over time, I began to embrace the trials and learn from them.

I often describe the trials I had endured and embraced as spiritual workouts. How does a muscle get stronger and grow? We add resistance that pushes against something, along with a lot of repetition. This is how we strengthen our spiritual muscles as well. One workout doesn't make a muscle strong. Repetition must come into play. So, each day, as I embraced these intense times of suffering, I could feel the repetition and resistance that I had to work against. It was difficult and often painful.

Like any new workout, I had to choose to stay focused on God and be disciplined in applying the training that He had already taught me. Being consistent while persevering in my trials, I could feel God continually walking with me and strengthening me as He dealt with the deeper matters of my heart.

As my roots of faith and trust grew deeper and deeper in God, I began to have a trust in Him that far outweighed the pain I was going through. Over time, I was able to consider it pure joy whenever I faced trials of any kind (James 1:2) because I knew God was working it all for my good (Romans 8:28). I knew He deeply loved me and wanted to set me free from the things that were holding me back from experiencing all that He had for me. However, my attitude was not always one of surrendering my heart fully to Him. But His deep love for me would bring me to a place of hungering for Him and His will.

Chapter 3

HUNGER FOR PEACE
AND TRUST IN GOD

My hunger for peace and trust in God began with the realization that the condition of my heart was deeply impacting *every* area of my life. And then I was reminded of a Bible study that I had attended many years ago.

The teacher had said, "I want you to read the parable of the four soils and share what you feel it means at our next Bible study session." As I read verse 4:13 in the parable found in Matthew, Mark, and Luke, the book of Mark stood out. There was one word that powerfully captured my attention. That word was *any.* Jesus was telling his disciples if they didn't understand this parable, how would they understand *any* parable. This got my attention and at that very moment, I wanted to understand and was eager and hungry to know more.

The parable reads: [3] "Listen! A farmer went out to sow his seed. [4] As he was scattering the seed, some fell along the path, and the birds came and ate it up. [5] Some fell on rocky places, where it did not have much soil. It sprang up quickly because the soil was shallow. [6] But when the sun came up, the plants were scorched, and they withered because they had no root. [7] Other seeds fell among thorns, which grew up and choked the plants so that they did not bear grain. [8] Still other seeds fell on good soil. It came up, grew, and produced a crop, some multiplying thirty, some sixty, some a hundred times." [13] Then Jesus said to them, "Don't you understand this parable? How then will you understand *any* parable?"

Jesus then explained the parable. [14] "The farmer sows the Word. [15] Some people are like seed along the path, where the Word is sown. As soon as they hear it, Satan comes and takes away the Word that was sown in them. [16] Others, like seed sown on rocky places, hear the Word and at once receive it with joy. [17] But since they have no root, they last only a short time. When trouble or persecution comes because of the Word, they quickly fall away. [18] Still others, like seed sown among thorns, hear the Word; [19] but the worries of this life, the deceitfulness of wealth and the desires for other things come in and choke the Word, making it unfruitful. [20] Others, like seed sown on good soil, hear the Word, accept it, and produce a crop—some thirty, some sixty, some a hundred times what was sown" (Mark 4:3-20 NIV).

Everything Flows from the Heart

As I meditated on the parable of the sower, I understood that the soil is my heart, and the seed is the Word of God. Then I questioned the condition of my heart's soil. Was the soil hard, shallow, rocky, thorny, weedy, or good and fertile? I couldn't help but think about the condition of my heart in relation to these scriptures. "For out of the abundance of the heart his mouth speaks" (Luke 6:45 ESV). "Above all else, guard your heart, for everything you do flows from it" (Proverbs 4:23). "For as he thinks in his heart, so is he" (Proverbs 23:7 NKJV).

God was showing me that everything flows from the heart and the condition of my heart (soil) deeply mattered. I wanted to know the condition of my heart and God simply told me to ask myself these questions as I go through life. "What is flowing out of you regularly, Abby?" "What are you thinking?" "What are you speaking?" He said the answers to those questions would show me the true condition of my heart. God was lovingly tending to my heart.

God Tends to My Heart

As I thought more about this parable, I reflected on a time when I was younger and having to help my parents prepare the garden each year for planting. The first thing we did was pick up the big rocks and sticks from the area where we were planting the garden. Then my dad would till the ground, and we would remove more rocks and weeds until it was cleared and ready for fertilizer. Only then could we plant the garden.

My mom would often say, "Make sure you get those weeds out by the roots or else they will grow back." Some weeds easily came out, but others did not. I would pull, but they wouldn't budge, so I would grab tightly and wiggle the weed and pull a little more. Sometimes that would help, but other times, the roots would not break free. I would then get my garden tools to break the ground up and wiggle the weed a little more. It was a back-and-forth tug-of-war with deep-rooted weeds, but finally, with effort, they would come out…roots and all.

Common sense would indicate that having a fruitful garden needs much preparation, which requires weeding, removing debris, and tilling the ground so that good seed can thrive in fertile soil. Only then can a garden reap a bountiful harvest.

As I studied this parable more deeply, I began to understand that if the garden of my heart held weeds and those hard rocky places of guilt, worry, anxiety, insecurity, or anything negative, how then could I plant healthy seeds.

The "debris" and the "weeds" had to be removed, so that the soil of my heart could be that good and fertile soil, ready to receive "seed" (the Word). If not, I would not be able to truly grasp and understand *any* of God's Word. Satan would then have an opened door to take the Word from me or choke it out of me, so it would not deeply root in my heart and bear good fruit. What a revelation!

While meditating on this revelation, these thoughts came to me: *Am I willing to let God have full access to every area of my heart? Am I willing to let Him be the Master Gardener and till up the hard places in my heart? Am I willing to let Him pull up the weeds and get rid of the rocks? Is my heart fertile? Will my life be fruitful? Will I reap a harvest?*

Good and Fertile Soil

After this deeper revelation, I prayed, "God, I want my heart to be good and fertile soil. Whatever is in my heart that is not of You, and whatever is standing between You and me, expose it and remove it. I deeply desire that people see You in me. I want my life to reflect who You are. I want others to see Your strength, steadiness, and stability as I go through life. My heart is fully surrendered to You. Have Your way in my life and be the Master Gardener who refines, purifies, and tends to all matters of my heart."

Years ago, I would have never had the courage to pray such a prayer. I was terrified of what might happen, what I might have to go through, or what would be exposed in my heart. I didn't want to be uncomfortable, and I certainly did NOT want to go through anything hard or intense...especially The Refiner's fire.

For years, fear paralyzed me, which eventually led to hitting rock bottom. I would never move forward in life when I felt fear. I believed it was a warning of danger, and I needed to stay where I was...where I was comfortable and safe. And so that is what I did. But something was wrong with that picture. Was my life's goal to be safe and comfortable?

The trials I endured and share in this book reveal God's constant prompting to do the uncomfortable and to be strong and courageous (Joshua 1:9). I remember when God spoke to my heart and said, "You cannot have courage without fear." That statement spoke loudly to me. I had to sit with that for a moment and ponder it. Then His still small voice proceeded to say, "If you truly want to be strong and courageous, then you are going to feel fear but don't let it stop you from moving forward. It doesn't take strength or courage to go the safe, comfortable, easy route. You are going to have to continually step out in faith despite any fear or uncomfortable feelings you may have. Remember I am always with you."

In walking out these intense seasons of trials, I leaned on God for strength and courage to move forward in what He was asking me to do. I was always ready and willing to do God's will. That didn't make it easier, but I knew God strengthens those whose hearts were fully committed to Him (2 Chronicles 16:9).

Some of the deep-rooted things in my heart that God wanted to deal with took a bit more time to remove by the roots. There was a time of a tugging back and forth.... peace and then no peace, trust in God, and then no trust in God. My heart's desire wanted to be unwavering, steady, stable, and to have peace that surpasses all understanding. I wanted to live from a deeper place of surrender and experience deeper freedom.

My heart was completely and fully committed and surrendered to Him, so He could have His way in me. I greatly desired, more than my comforts, to reflect on who He is. With that deep desire, it would require letting Him deal with the deeper matters of my heart because everything that I am, and everything I do and say flows from my heart. I didn't want to get to heaven and hear God tell me that I had missed His very best, because I played it safe in wanting the easy, comfortable route, and all because I had allowed fear to paralyze me. Instead, I wanted and still want to hear, "Well done, good and faithful servant." So, keep refining me God, until all they see is You in me.

Chapter 4

THE TRIALS BEGIN

Summer 2010: A Stirring in Tim's Heart

I was pregnant with our son Shia (pronounced Shy-uh) when my husband felt a stirring in his heart to make a career change so he could provide better for us. To my surprise, he mentioned joining the military. He had never mentioned anything about the military during our marriage of nine years. Trembling in fear, I remembered many years prior being in a dressing room and overhearing a lady in the next dressing room talking about her husband getting ready for deployment. As I listened, fear swept over me and I thought, *There is no way I could ever do*

that. I had that same thought when Tim mentioned the military, *There is no way I can do that.*

God exposed something deeper in my heart... another layer of fear, so I could experience the fullness that God had for me; I needed to let Him tend to that area of my heart. I needed to let Him till the ground of my heart so He could set me free.

Fall 2010: Shia is Born

Tim had not yet moved forward with joining the military, but that was the direction he felt he must take. Now I was giving birth to our son, Shia, which his name means "gift from God." In the middle of pushing, I was having thoughts that Tim would be leaving for basic training at some point, and I would be left alone with our precious, new son. This was our first child, so the thought  of being alone without Tim was overwhelming and terrifying. I did not feel ready for this change in our lives.

Tim was completely in love with his son, and they bonded beautifully right from the start. Shia was four days old, and I clearly remember standing in our kitchen and Tim coming up to me and saying, "I am not going to join the military. It doesn't feel like now is the time." I didn't ask any questions. I was just so relieved that I held him and cried.

Following Shia's birth, I was still working part-time in our home as a massage therapist. Not long after Tim told me that he would not be joining the military, God brought some new clients to me who had varying military experiences. Plus, some of the regular clients, who had years of military experience talked about their time in service.

One of my regular clients had served in the Army for over 20 years. I also had another regular client that was a spouse of a military man who had served for over 20 years. A few other clients had family members serving in the military as well. I didn't think much of it then, but considering I had heard numerous stories about their military journeys and had asked so many questions about their experiences, the military was constantly in my thoughts, despite Tim not joining the Army. What was God doing? Was He preparing my heart for what was to happen next?

Tim still had a deep stirring in his heart that something needed to change so he could provide better for our family. Many months later, Tim mentioned joining the police academy. Because of the danger, his announcement caused me to have some fear, but at least he wouldn't be separated from me. After some time in prayer, we felt that Tim's next step was to join the police academy.

Fall 2011: Tim Joins the Police Academy

While Tim was training in the police academy, I was trying to wrap my head around the dangers he might face. I reached out to a friend who had been a police officer for a very long time and shared some of my fears with him. The biggest takeaway from our conversation was that Tim would be well trained and would rely on his training. At that moment, I felt like God was saying, "You too, will have to rely on your training and remember how I have taught you to walk this out with peace."

Tim graduated and proceeded to look for a job, but the door was not opening. It was not because Tim was not qualified. It was because God had a different plan. Door after door was not opening and I knew deep in my heart our next step, and I knew Tim knew as well. However, it was a subject that we did not yet talk about.

We kept trying to force this police officer's door open. During this time weird things started happening that got our attention. Tim was working as a deputy reserve and was told he was next in line to get hired. He showed up to the meeting to hear the announcement of the new deputy and was shocked that it wasn't him. Apparently, Tim never received the email communication regarding the position, so they assumed he was no longer interested and gave it to the next person in line. This was very disappointing and a gut punch to both of us.

One day, Tim and I went for a walk. While pushing our son in the stroller, I asked Tim if there was anything he could do, what would that be? I honestly wanted to know if he had the choice and could be a police officer anywhere, what would be his chosen location. But that is not what came out of his mouth. His answer surprised me, "I would join the Army." What surprised me more was my reply, "Then you should do that."

What was I saying? That was not what I really wanted. I knew that path would separate us. I would be without my husband and my son would be without his daddy for who knew how long. We didn't talk about it anymore, but I knew both of us understood the sacrifices that would come in taking that step.

Shortly after that conversation, Tim proceeded to keep trying to open the door to work as a police officer. We thought maybe we were supposed to relocate and be closer to his family. So, he checked to see if Oklahoma City was hiring, and they were. We thought maybe this was going to be the open door.

Tim called and was told that they would be sending information regarding the next steps to get hired through email and mail. After a few weeks, Tim called to touch base regarding the information he was supposed to receive. They said they had sent it out. Yet again, he did not receive anything, so he missed the date.

I had been sitting on the floor in the living room and listening to the entire conversation. He then asked when the next hiring date would be, and they told tell him that they were currently not hiring. We both just looked at each other. Tim said, "Babe, that door is shut." And I responded softly, knowing what was next for us... "I know." Then he said, "I have to join the Army." With a sigh of deep resignation, I said again, "I know."

He just held me while I cried, but I had an even deeper peace because I knew that I knew that God was directing our steps. The entire time, we had prayed that God would shut doors that were not of Him, because we desired to be on the path that He wanted for us. He did indeed shut the door.

Chapter 5

A DIFFERENT LIFE

Fall 2012: Tim Joins the Army

Tim joined the Army and over the next couple of months, we experienced what we were not ready for…a lack of support. We had so many friends and family members speaking against what

we were about to do. There were times when it was hard to stand up against the opposition, but we were so grateful that the doors had been closed for the police officer jobs. We knew that God had stepped in and shut those doors. And it was God who sent the right clients to me to prepare my heart for military life. We knew we must not be swayed in our decision. We had to follow God and not man's opinion.

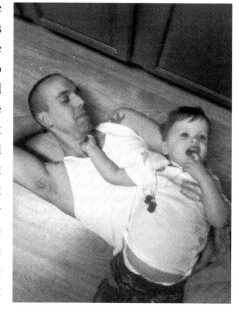

Early 2013: Tim Leaves for Basic Training

I remember the night before Tim was supposed to leave for basic training. We were holding each other while lying in bed. Neither one wanted to be apart. We asked God if this could somehow pass us, but then we both told God it was not our will but His will that we desired. The next day, with tears in our eyes, we said our goodbyes. Thus, began our military journey.

My feelings were overwhelming. I was numb, in a daze, and struggling, so I reached out to my friend, Cherie. She offered words of encouragement with her message:

"I am constantly where you are. Letting go is the hardest thing to do, yet it is one of the greatest lessons in faith. I've learned that it's less about my trivial circumstances and more about my flesh being crucified so that I might reflect Christ in greater ways. Christ is IN you. Allow Him to reign. Let His peace consume you through the spiritual battles and ask yourself this question in EVERY single situation, 'What would you do/say if you were ABSOLUTELY confident God was with you???' Rest in Him. He's teaching you that you can trust Him even when everything in life says that you can't. You are in the school of faith…and I'm in the class with you :). Fight the good fight and never take your eyes off Jesus. Hugs."

Over the next several months while our little family was separated, God began to expose so many things within my heart. The biggest issue was that my security was dependent on Tim being home. Until you are put in the unfamiliar, you truly don't know where your security rests.

If you read my first book, *Living Still,* you know that I had a long history of suffering intense anxiety, which eventually led me to hit rock bottom. I could feel some anxiety surfacing and my joy slipping away because of my separation from Tim. I knew it was okay to miss him, but for me to be completely toppled over by it and not be able to function meant that I had put Tim above God. The intensity of this season of my life was exposing what was in my heart.

As I chose to surrender and embrace the new season we were in, I could feel God teaching me that He was my source of joy and peace and not Tim. It was a painful season of letting go and trusting on a deeper level than I had ever experienced. I had to learn to walk this out with God as my source.

Spring 2013: Walk with Me

While Tim was away, I pondered all that would be in our future…relocation, deployment, potential danger, leaving all that I knew behind, and stepping into a completely new life. It was overwhelming, and honestly, I did not want to do it.

One night, I was taking some time to put into practice being still with God, when a scene played in my mind. I saw myself locking hands with Jesus, but He was slowly dragging me down a road. I wasn't resisting Him, but I was looking backward as He was walking forwards. He gently spoke into my spirit, "You are going this direction with Me, but I would rather you willingly get up and walk with Me, rather than having to drag you. I have so much for you. Trust me. Stand up and walk with Me…hand in hand. Don't focus on the entire journey because that will overwhelm you. Just trust that I will take you through each step."

That scene was very accurate. I felt like I was moving forward with God, but I was making it difficult, because I was holding tight to what was comfortable and what I knew, rather than leaving it behind and stepping into the unknown. And though I had a tight grip on what was comfortable, I wasn't experiencing any peace. After understanding this, I felt a powerful shift in my heart and felt

God give me the strength and courage to stand up and face this, knowing that He was walking hand in hand with me. It would take courage, but I wanted to deeply trust Him.

This picture of my son and me was taken by my brother-in-law during the time Tim was in basic training. He wasn't aware of the scene that had played out in my mind, but this picture is a reminder of that moment God told me to stand up, trust Him, and walk hand in hand with Him. I printed and framed that picture and put it where I could see it every day as an encouragement to keep walking and trusting.

Spring 2013: I Surrender

Shia was using my phone to listen to music on YouTube when he managed to find a song I had never heard. This wasn't something he normally did. The song, "I Surrender," by Hillsong

Worship, began to play. Shia wanted to listen to this song over and over, so we listened several times a day while daddy was gone. Every time the song played, certain words in the lyrics stood out. Words about surrendering myself, wanting to know God more and allowing Him to have His way resonated deep within my heart and soul. (I Surrender can be heard on YouTube.)

Surrendering to God was exactly what our family was doing. What a beautiful blessing of encouragement for God to lead my precious Shia, who was only two, to find this song that spoke so deeply to my heart and reminded me to keep the posture of a surrendered heart, so He could have His way in me every day. It was truly powerful.

Summer 2013: Graduation from Basic Training

Tim graduated from basic training. Seeing him for the first time after so many months was amazing and beautiful. I didn't know what to expect because we had never been apart that long. I was filled with excitement, eagerness, and nervousness, but we picked right back up from where we had been before he left.

During our entire journey, Tim and I had been concerned about his relationship with Shia. They had a beautiful bond that we did not want broken, but God protected it, and it was as though they never missed a beat.

Summer 2013: Orders to Hawaii

After basic training, Tim received orders for his first duty station, which would be Hawaii. As much as I trusted God, I could feel that He was exposing my deep love for the comfort of my home and all my Missouri roots where I was born and raised. I had friends, family, a church I loved, my business, clients, and community involvement. There was so much that I was about to step away from, and it was painful. My grip was tight, but I knew I had to let go and trust God.

Tim had to go ahead of us to Hawaii, so I was left to tend to the movers packing our household goods and then traveling alone with Shia to Hawaii. Shia had never flown before and it was going to be a very long day of flying.

I was surprised that I didn't cry when leaving Branson, Missouri. I was just so excited that soon we would all be together as a family that I wasn't focused on the pain of leaving everything and everyone behind as much as I was focused on being back with Tim.

Chapter 6

DIFFICULTY ADJUSTING

Arrival in Hawaii

Shia did great on the flights. He slept some, we played some, and he watched his favorite movie, "Cars" on his iPad.

Tim picked us up from the airport in a rental car to take us to our new townhome, which was located on the Army post. But as we got closer to post, a sudden and intense shift happened inside of me. Tears cascaded down my cheeks as I became overwhelmed with the reality of the move.

Everything was different. Nothing was familiar. Our household goods would not be arriving for six to eight weeks. The only familiar things we had were what we carried in our suitcases. The temporary furniture that the military provided was covered in thick plastic. I was deeply uncomfortable, and I already missed my home in Branson.

We got settled, but with the major time change and the long day of flying, Shia and I were exhausted, so we took a little nap. When I awoke, reality hit me again, and I felt like I needed to take a walk to put into practice my training to take time and be still with God.

Hawaii is beautiful, and I am so grateful that God placed me in such a beautiful place for Him to take care of the deeper places in my heart that needed tending. He is so gracious like that. He knows my love for nature.

During the walk, I saw a beautiful tree that looked like a huge umbrella. I stood under it in complete awe of its beauty, and as I looked up, I heard God's still small voice encouraging me, "I will hide you under the shadows of My wing (Psalm 17:8). Trust me during this season. I have pruned you back, so you can be more fruitful (John 15:2). I am also cutting away things within you that aren't bearing any fruit."

This is a picture of the "umbrella" tree. Isn't it beautiful? I would love to say that I had rejoiced and fully embraced God's pruning process, but I didn't…not at all. I felt incredibly depressed and isolated as I struggled to adjust to Hawaii, Army life, and just things in general.

Encouragement from Matt

I reached out for prayer and shared my heart with my dear friends, Matt and Becca. Matt replied with a beautiful text that encouraged me and confirmed within my heart that God was doing a deep work in me.

Matt told me that God digs deeper within us. Not so that we will be stuck, but so that we can be free. Free from those things that hinder us, thereby freeing us from past hurts and wounds that have caused us to believe lies in our thoughts and eventually in our hearts. He frees us from our own standards and expectations that we set for ourselves, but are impossible to reach, because they were made by us to control. But God has so much more for us, and so much better, because His ways are much higher than our ways. God is *not* looking at us and saying, "You should be standing stronger and doing better. You're not measuring up." Instead, He is saying, "I love you; let go. I will carry you, for I am making you new. I am doing a good work in you." It is God working, not us.

Matt went on to say, "Oh, the deep digging He has been doing this week in me as well. Uncovering some very deep-rooted, self-worth issues and toxic thought patterns. Although it has been painful, He is helping me see the root of those toxic patterns and those things that He is freeing me from.

Thinking about you, my sweet friend, and feeling so much of His deep love for you and knowing that He is doing that deep work in you as well. He wants to finish that perfect work within us so we will lack nothing. Love you very much."

Too Expensive to go Back Home

Looking back, I understand why God had to put me on an island, making it very expensive to leave. If I had been stateside, most certainly, I would have left numerous times to return home to Missouri. I remember crying out often to God, "I just want to go home!" I was deeply uncomfortable and wanted to go back to the things I knew.

This new transition was hard, but I knew God had me right where I was supposed to be. I could feel myself fighting against it and having a hard time embracing it. But even in my resisting, God so beautifully spoke to me, "Home is wherever I have placed you. I am your home."

God knew what He was doing. He had set the stage perfectly, so I would be forced to dive in deeper and allow Him to deal with the impurities that were surfacing and being exposed during my intense trial.

I Have no Worth

During that time, when things were being cut away, I remember deeply believing that I had no worth and value. I was not working anymore, despite my efforts to transfer my massage therapy license to Hawaii. I needed more schooling to meet their state requirements. I was not involved in the community, despite my efforts to get involved, but having a young son and with Tim working, it was very difficult to engage in anything else. Neither were we involved in any church community despite efforts to find the right church. I felt like I was drowning.

Fall 2013: "Oceans" Was Released

The song "Oceans" by United, was released in the Fall of 2013. Shia loved that song, as did I. It was played on repeat for a while in our home. And often in the mornings, while Shia was eating breakfast, we played a video with the song.

When I first heard "Oceans," I cried. I felt like it was written just for me. God has a way of using music to pull me close to Him. Sometimes I don't have words to express what I am feeling and then to discover a song that speaks directly to me is powerful and so encouraging. Every word of this song penetrated my heart and ministered to me. I connected deeply to it because it was my heart's cry during this time in my life.

The words of this song revealed a special truth as God awakened within my heart the need to focus on Him and not the storms around me. He was gently calling me to step out upon the

waves of life, while keeping my eyes focused on Him. He would
be my guide and strength as He took me into a deeper walk of faith
with Him. I knew I could trust Him because my heart, and all that
I am, belonged to Him. (I encourage you to listen to "Oceans" on
YouTube.)

As I began to stop fighting against everything and began to
fully surrender and embrace life as it was, I could hear God
speaking more clearly. He said, "Your worth and value are not in
the things I have you doing, but they are found in Me alone. Your
joy is found in Me alone as well. If I took everything from you,
Abby, would I be enough?"

That was hard to hear, but if I was being honest at that moment,
my answer would have been, "No." I had previously found so
much joy in the comforts of my life as they were, in my career,
having family and friends close by, and being involved in a church
and the community. All of that had taken the place of a rich, deep
joy that God wanted me to experience in having Him in my life. A
deep work was being done in my heart. How could I be truly stable
and steady in life if my joy came from external things that come
and go?

God's pruning was very difficult, but the revelation and
growth that occurred as I walked fully surrendered, hand in hand
with God, allowed Him to go deeper and deeper into my heart. It
was powerful. Had my life stayed the same in Missouri, I would
have never known or experienced such joy, as I anchored more
deeply into Him.

I pondered God's great love for me as He was purifying my
heart and helping my roots grow deeper and deeper into Him. It
was as though He needed to take me out of the game of the life
that I was living, despite my efforts to do things "for" God. It was
hard, and I felt many times that I was just sitting on the bench with
God-given gifts and talents and not using them to serve Him. At

times, I felt all the emotions of laziness, guilt, pressure, and an obligation to somehow get back in the game.

I Had a Dream

During this time, I began to have the same dream at night. I continued to have this dream until the year 2021 when it changed, which I will share later.

The dream involved my senior year basketball coach and team. I played basketball in high school and was pretty good. I was a starter my senior year and never sat the bench except to rest or if we were winning by a lot.

In the dream, a basketball game is going on, but I am sitting the bench and not playing at all during the game. I am eagerly watching the game, ready to play, so I keep saying, "Put me in, Coach."

This dream reflected so much of how I felt during that time in my life. I wanted to get back into the game of teaching, encouraging, speaking, and being used by God to fulfill those things I knew I was called to do. Instead, I sat in Hawaii doing none of that; however, something better was happening. God was deeply refining and working on the matters of my heart that were not of Him. He was purifying me while I "sat the bench," so I could be an even greater "player" for God.

Chapter 7

CHANGES TO BE MADE

Early 2014: Simplifying Our Living

Tim felt a stirring in his heart that we needed to move off post and downsize considerably to pay off more of our debt. We had only been on the island for five months when this stirring happened. Our household goods and vehicle had finally arrived, and I was just getting used to our new home. I wasn't ready to let go of more things. Despite my feelings, we proceeded to look for places off post.

Nothing felt like the right place, until we looked at a small 700 square-foot condo. As soon as we walked through the door, we both felt like this was where we belonged. What I liked so much about the condo was the color of the walls. They reminded me of the colors of the walls in our Branson home that we had sold prior to moving to Hawaii.

I really liked the new area. There was a pool, hot tub, and two little parks on-site, and just down the street was another beautiful park. The sidewalks along the street would be perfect for Shia and me to take long walks together and for me to run. I was hoping God would open the door because many people had applied.

The landlord called and told us we were chosen, and I was so excited. I guess I was more ready for this change than I had thought, or perhaps it was just a jolt from God to help me with the next step. And that was letting go of a lot of stuff, so we could fit into the very small condo.

God Winks

The condo had a little balcony with a storage closet. As I was putting some of our things in the closet, I found a rock. It was not just any rock; it was a rock that had a center that looked like a heart. If you have read my first book, *Living Still*, then you know that God often speaks to me through hearts. I felt like this was something He had placed in this closet just for me. Those little God winks reassured me that we were exactly where we were supposed to be and that each day, He was walking with us.

Adjusting to Military Life

Prior to leaving Missouri, a military man's spouse told me something that I have applied many times in many areas of my life. I love how God so graciously allowed me to hear this as He knew it would help me along my journey while adjusting to military life. She said, "Keep a loose grip on everything."

Military life is always changing, and because schedules are always changing, Tim is gone for a lot of training missions. Deployments come quickly. There is standby for potential deployment, and plans change in the middle of plans. You must keep a loose grip on all things related to the Army, or you will absolutely go insane.

At first, that was a difficult adjustment for both of us. It wasn't a life that we were used to, and I quickly discovered that I liked the comfort of having a plan and sticking to it when it involved our lives. Now I can adjust to traffic jams, long lines at the grocery store, etc., but unexpected drastic changes in our lives, are an entirely different thing. With each unexpected event that occurred with military life, things were being exposed in my heart that I didn't like, and I knew that God wanted to tend to them. I had a big grip on my life, my plans, and my schedule, and with each sudden change, my peace would leave.

Tim frequently had training missions that would come up, and then he would have training missions that would be scheduled and then suddenly change. One mission required that he leave for three months. He packed and prepared to leave and was out the door. Less than 12 hours later, he was back home. Talk about an emotional roller coaster. Having to say goodbye and then have him return so quickly did a number on me. I could hear God say, "Trust Me. Flow with Me. Have peace in Me, not your schedule. Be content in all things."

I also remember several different occasions where there was talk about dangerous deployments that were potentially going to occur. I trembled in fear thinking of the possibility of Tim leaving to fight in combat. Each time we talked about this, my heart raced, and my mind was consumed with fear.

You might think that my fear would be a normal reaction to the situation, and I should give myself some grace. I agree with you to a point…but then again, my heart yearned to be steady and stable in all storms. I wanted to trust God deeply and this was just a deeper layer of fear that God was exposing and wanting to bring to my attention.

My friend, Becca, texted some encouragement during this time in my journey:

> "I cannot imagine the testing. I know that God is diving deeper in you, refreshing you in the truth that He is your security — not Tim, not Shia, not family. God has had to refresh this truth in me, too!! Some serious fire, but it will bring some serious shine!! You are not going backwards, just deeper. You don't have control, but He does. I am most definitely praying because I know I would be very challenged as well if I were going through it."

God reminded me again that my comfort and security must be in Him and not Tim. I must trust God's plans for our lives and that we would always be in the right place at the right time because our steps are ordered by Him.

Truthfully, I felt like I was going to be abandoned on this island, and I was retracing feelings from my childhood involving fears of being alone. Even though God had healed me from some past deep-rooted anxiety, there was yet another layer He was exposing and wanting to heal. I had never been put in this type of situation.... this type of refiner's fire.... but there I was, sitting in it, and fear was surfacing.

God reminded me of what He had told me while I was under that umbrella tree. "I will hide you in the shadows of My wings." He was comforting me, saying, "I have you close to Me. I know this is hard, but I am here. I will never abandon you. I will never leave you or forsake you" (Hebrew 13:5AMP). Did I really trust that? Was the truth in God's Word really anchored deep within my heart? It wasn't, because my circumstances were choking out that truth; therefore, there was no real depth in my heart for that seed of truth to grow and become fruitful, just like the parable of the soil.

Tim Leaves for Another Country

Each time Tim was called away and I was alone with Shia, it was an opportunity — a spiritual workout — to grow and get stronger. I had many opportunities because he was gone a lot. I had to decide if I would sit defeated and feel sorry for myself, or would I embrace the circumstances, step into them, press into God, and trust Him.

I remember when Tim was deployed for the first time, and I felt completely abandoned on the island. So, I reached out to share my heart with my Missouri friend, Deneé. The following is our text message conversation:

Abby – "I see what God is doing. He is pulling me in closer to have complete security in Him. Right now, I am sitting here facing it. Looking at it square in the face. This is where all the fear started as a little kid. Being alone...feeling abandoned. Now here I am on this island, stripped of all comforts, security, familiar things, etc. My flesh wants to rise up and fight. Old feelings are trying to resurface BUT I know who lives in me. I know Jesus is working intensely and He is right here with me."

Deneé – "Wow, Abby. That's the key. You're seeing the past, the plan, and the purpose. Stay close. Let the intensity of His Presence vibrate the doubt and fear away so that you experience a whole newness in stillness. Heaven on earth. His Kingdom in you always."

Abby – "Why is it so painful? I had no idea this was still in me. I want it out. I want freedom."

Deneé – "He is the great physician. A surgeon with the best hands and best perspective. Trust Him to remove what is ready to be pruned. You don't have to understand it all right now. Just trust Him and let Him do His part. The rest of you will flourish from the pruning."

She then texted me this beautiful prophetic Word from the Lord:

"I am so proud of you, daughter of the Most High. Your gentle spirit. Your warrior way. I crafted you for this time and season and through your pruning, I will do mighty things for My Kingdom on earth. You are called. You have answered, and I am equipping you for these mighty things. I do not ask you to go an easy way. I ask you to go the needed way. My lost people. My beloved. I cry to them in the night and call them unto Me. Will you shepherd the lost and broken Abby, My beloved daughter? I will be your guide. I will be your lamp. I will be your armor-bearer. I am the Great Servant. I will because I Am, and I do great things. You are My beloved and I am yours. I will nurture you and protect you. I will because I Am, and My Word Is true. Abba Father."

It was the exact jolt I needed to stand up and keep persevering, with my attention completely focused on God and not on the painful trial. As I embraced and stepped into it, God worked, and my spiritual roots grew deeper in Him. Over time, when Tim was absent from us, I felt stronger and more peaceful, steady, and stable.

Embracing Shia's Quirky Behaviors

During the many adjustments, our son, Shia, was not talking. At three, he hadn't really begun to talk. He had progressed with everything else normally but talking was an area of growth where he never progressed. Tim is a very quiet man. He often said that he wouldn't talk if he didn't have to. So, at first, we just thought Shia was taking after his daddy.

Shia had a few quirky things he did during this time that were different, but we didn't give them much thought. Shia was a happy child, full of laughter, and was healthy. We just assumed that in time, he would grow out of his quirky behaviors and begin to start talking, but he never did.

With each passing day, month, and year, Shia never communicated verbally with us, and things began to surface in my heart. Yet again, another refiner's fire was needed for God to tend to the matters that were even deeper in my heart. I desperately wanted to be free from those things that I allowed to trouble me, so I was willing to walk in obedience with God so He could work in me.

I think that parents who suspect that something is wrong with their child are initially in denial of there being a problem. I know I was. I wanted Shia to be a typical child, but he wasn't. I was having a very hard time embracing it all, and at first, I kept resisting the thought of something being different about Shia and was hoping that the situation would change. I had such a tight grip on what I wanted and living in such denial, that I had completely lost my peace.

I would think and wonder if I might have done something to cause this, even though I had a very healthy pregnancy and was not a vaccinator. The home birth was problem-free, and I delivered a very healthy Shia. I breastfed him for over two years and made his baby food. I also fed him as much organic food as we could afford. I didn't give him sugar until he was two, and the list of precautions was endless.

What could I have forgotten? What might I have done to cause this? I felt overwhelmed with guilt and consumed with trying to figure out how and why this had happened. I wanted it all to go away and continue life with a typical child.

I researched and researched, which only led to fear, worry, guilt, and more denial. I had no idea how to be a mother to a special needs child, and I was fighting against that reality. I was not embracing the possible reality, and I was not trusting God. I was exerting my own strength and effort and not relying on God for comfort or guidance. And I was not relying on my training to be still. I became obsessed with trying to fix it all, convinced that a good mother would fix what was wrong. But the underlying, deep-rooted issue was perfectionism, insecurities, comparison, lack of trust in God's plan, control issues, and caring about what people thought.

Truth Spoken with Love

I remember so clearly when I was sitting on the floor in our condo in Hawaii. My thoughts were racing with fear and worry, and I asked my husband, "What is wrong with Shia?" Tim looked me straight in the eyes and firmly said, "Nothing is wrong with him. He is not the problem. You are."

Tim only saw Shia as perfect and amazing, just the way God made him. Here I was overtaken by fear and fighting against it all. Tim was embracing it and walking in peace and enjoying Shia. Never had Tim spoken those words, but they went straight to my heart because he was right and they were spoken with love. It shook me awake and caused me to let go of the tight grip that I had on everything related to Shia.

That memorable day, I felt God begin to work deeper in my heart, and I surrendered. I was able to find a sense of footing again as I went back to my training to be still and trust God. I knew I needed to give myself grace as I learned to walk this journey with God. Instead of constant researching and trying to take matters into my own hands, I began to rely more on God to guide me in the way He trained me.

I felt God's Presence so close as I began to grieve the loss of a "normal" child and embrace Shia. I would need to let go of the tight grip of normalcy because having such a grip on something you desperately want only causes more pain. God met me where I was and began to encourage and guide me.

There was much work to be done in my heart since I had fully surrendered my hopes and dreams for our son to the Master Gardener. As God continued tilling the soil of my heart, I was able to see things a bit more clearly. I began to see more clearly that children are God's gift.

Chapter 8

God's Loving Instruction

Children Are a Gift

As God was bringing things to the surface and exposing them, He shared the truth that children are a gift. We believed that Shia was God's gift to us. That was why the meaning of Shia's name, "Gift from God," was so important to us. Unfortunately, my attitude towards His gift was that of a bratty child. He then reminded me of how I used to act as a young child at Christmas.

I would open a gift from my parents, and if it was not what I wanted, I would have a bratty attitude and complain instead of being thankful. Remembering my childish and selfish behavior grieved my heart greatly because I did not want to be this way. It confirmed even more that there was a great deal of work that needed to be done in my heart.

Having truth revealed is always painful, but I knew that the only way the deeper things could be healed was to bring them to the surface and let God tend to them. His correction wasn't for the purpose of condemning or shaming. In His great love, He was setting me free from those things that would bring deep pain.

Growth in the Lord is Hard

Tim was injured while doing some training and had to have shoulder surgery. On our way home from his surgery, we became stuck in a traffic jam. At the beginning of the traffic jam, Tim was throwing up from the anesthesia...thankfully not in the car. For hours, the traffic was thick and barely moving. For long periods of time, we were at a standstill with nothing moving. The situation was completely out of my control; however, my response was in my control. I chose to remain calm and peaceful.

Shia and Tim were asleep for a couple of hours, so I took advantage of the stillness with God, and He began speaking to my heart:

> "This traffic jam is much like your journey in life as you are growing in Me. Little by little, I chisel away the junk

within you. It takes time and lots of patience as you trust Me, the Master Gardener, to tend to the areas of your heart that need tending. Sometimes you feel you are moving at a snail's pace in life, while other times you feel you aren't moving or progressing forward at all."

There were times during that traffic jam, that I gained speed up to 20 mph. It would give me hope that it was over, but then the traffic would slow again to a stop and then slowly move five miles per hour. At that point, I wanted to cry in frustration. No one likes to be slowed down in life when you are just gaining some momentum. But I regained my focus and reminded myself to stay calm and peaceful. Then God began speaking again.

"In your journey of growth, little flood gates of My blessings open up to you. Their purpose is to give you hope and strength to keep moving forward, growing in Me, then right back to what appears that you aren't progressing or moving at all. But you are. I am working. Little by little I am refining you to become more like Me in every way. It takes time and great patience as you trust Me to tend to the deeper matters of your heart that stand between you and Me and that are ultimately harming you."

Suddenly, after much time having passed, and sitting under pressure and frustration, the four-lane traffic thinned out and traffic began to flow. It began moving from five miles per hour to the regular speed limit of 55 miles per hour. I was so grateful and relieved that I cried. We had been sitting in that traffic jam for over five hours…a trip that was only supposed to take 30 minutes! In my amazement and gratitude, as traffic was flowing, God spoke to me.

"In the right timing, My flood gates will open in abundance to you. When you least expect it...suddenly...in the right timing...it will open, and you will know without a shadow of a doubt that it is Me. Trust Me. Wait on Me. I am faithful."

Growth in the Lord is hard. Being patient as God was refining not only me but also Tim, was painfully difficult. We wanted it over. We wanted it fixed now. We didn't want to wait. The uncomfortable feelings were intense with everything that we were going through.

One night while we were lying in bed talking, Tim was processing if he should sign another contract with the Army. With him home and healing from his injury, he was concerned about his military future. He had joined the Army at age 33. He was having doubts that his body would be able to keep up with the demands of a military career. He started doubting his path and said that maybe we should return to Branson after his three years were finished. He thought that it might be better if Shia and I had family and friends close to us.

I did feel alone and isolated, so I was tempted to give in and encourage him not to sign another contract. Instead, I replied that my training was not to make decisions based on emotions. I believed that God was speaking through me and saying that we were both vulnerable and not in a good place to make decisions at that time, so I said, "Let's wait until we are both more peaceful and then talk about this again."

Hurry up!

"Hurry up!" were the words that came out of a mom's mouth when her little girl, maybe age six, paused briefly to smile and wave at Shia and me as we passed her during our walk. My heart was immediately saddened as I pondered that moment:

> *I wonder how many times this little girl hears the words, "Hurry up, let's go, come on, move it." If it is frequently, I wonder if this mom knows that she is potentially programming her young child to always be moving at a faster pace and to be in a hurry throughout life. I wonder if this little girl will ever get to stop and smell the roses, feel the rain on her face, stare at the stars in the sky, wave at a smiling stranger like Shia and me, or will she have to always move at the faster pace of her parents.*

I am a "stop and smell the roses" kind of a person, but as I would watch Shia, he would observe nature and take things in more than I would. He is never in a hurry. I feel God uses Shia and his natural love to explore things in nature to slow me down and be even more still. It is something I need to embrace so that I can continue my journey.

Don't Root-Bound Shia

I was watching Shia play outside one day when I heard God speak into my spirit, "Don't root-bound Shia." I immediately remembered all the times I had transplanted plants with my mom that were root-bound. We would remove the plant from the pot and find the roots twisted and bound together. Carefully, we would unbind the roots and transplant the plant into a bigger pot so it could thrive and grow. My mom told me that if the plant was not transplanted into a larger pot, its roots would become so tightly bound, that the plant would slowly suffocate and die.

My mom's words and God's nudging caused me to think about Shia and how his roots could become bound if I kept him in such a small pot that he was not able to grow. God then proceeded to tell me that I needed to create boundaries for Shia but to make sure those boundaries...the pot...would be big enough for him to grow and thrive as God intended.

I thought about how much Shia loved to explore and climb; he had been venturing into wanting to climb trees. Because of my fears, I would resist him climbing too much, despite Shia having proven that he was an excellent and safe climber on the playgrounds. My fears were keeping him in that smaller "pot," where I believed he would be safe and where I would be comfortable. But then I felt God's nudging to let Shia climb those trees and expand his boundaries. I needed to provide a larger "pot" for him to thrive and grow.

Get in Shia's World

The more I surrendered and embraced the journey God had for me with the military and the issues with Shia, the more I could feel God tending to the deeper matters of my heart. Layer by layer, He was loving me enough to heal those areas of my heart, so I could experience deeper freedom in Him. Though I lacked confidence in my capabilities to mother a child who didn't talk, God would often guide me to just sit and watch Tim and Shia interact.

Tim being a man of few words allowed him to have a very special relationship with Shia. He understood Shia in a deeper way than I could. As I watched Tim interact with Shia, I noticed that Tim always got on Shia's level. He never had an agenda of what he wanted to do with Shia. He simply entered Shia's world to enjoy his presence. If people were around, Tim never cared what they thought of him or Shia.

I remember one day we were walking around Walmart. Shia loved the coolness of the tile floor, so he laid down on the floor in the middle of the aisle. To my surprise, Tim laid down on the floor with him. I just watched them. I took a picture to remember the freedom that Tim lived in with our son. He was fully engaged in Shia's world, not caring about the world around him. I later asked him why he did that and he said, "I wanted to be with my son."

Change My Approach

At this point, we planned to homeschool Shia, so the pressure to teach was all on me. I was sharing my concerns with Tim about Shia not grasping what I was trying to teach him, and he responded by telling me to change my approach.

Tim always understood how to enter Shia's world and allow Shia to play first. Tim would then present something like a puzzle or a toy. He was completely okay if Shia didn't engage with the toy, but most times, Shia would play with the toy.

What Tim did was simple, but I was making it too hard. I was trying to control things too much instead of just flowing with Shia and discovering something new and a different way to approach teaching Shia. I began applying this method, and I soon saw an entirely different world with Shia.

I continued to let go of control and embrace more fully my nonverbal child. When I did, I saw a shift happen within me. I began to understand Shia so much more…his body language and all his nonverbal cues that were his own language, which we called "Shia-nese." All of those communicated so much to me. I had been so focused on getting him to do things my way and make him talk, that I couldn't see anything else. I marveled as I watched Shia explore his world more deeply.

I was seeing this unique gift that God gave me being unwrapped ever so slowly. It was beautiful to discover more of who Shia was, so I prayed a lot for help to be the mother that Shia needed. As I prayed, God began to build my confidence. The spiritual workout of entering Shia's world each day strengthened my confidence and helped with some of my insecurities.

I was not there yet. There was more tugging and pulling God had to do to get the deeper-rooted things out of my heart. I was finding my groove when it was just the three of us, but more surfaced in my heart when I was out in public with Shia and other people would ask questions about Shia. "Why doesn't he talk?" "Can he talk?" "What's wrong with him?" "What happened to him?" "Why does he do that?" "Can he hear?" "Is he special?" I didn't know how to respond.

Many of the questions were difficult and hurtful. People would even comment on how I was doing things. One comment that was said a few times was, "He is too big for a stroller." What they didn't know was that Shia loved to be out in nature and to take long walks while riding in his stroller. I enjoyed it as well, but I almost stopped our fun excursions because of the invasive and insensitive comments.

Making Comparisons

There were times when I felt like a complete failure as a mom. I compared my son to others and myself to other moms. I was sure I was doing everything wrong. I was distracted by all the questions, the negative opinions, and the looks from others. My mind was beginning to fill with doubt, fear, frustration, and confusion. I felt very insecure and lacked so much confidence as a mother. It was overwhelming, and honestly, all the voices questioning and people staring made me want to stay home where I felt comfortable and safe, so I wouldn't have to deal with any of it.

I couldn't find that deep place of stillness, yet I knew I must find it, so, I kept pressing in. That is what I call it when it is harder for me to quiet my mind of all the noise of so many voices and connect with God's still small voice—that deep intuition given by God's Spirit. When I finally quieted my mind, His guidance that I needed forever changed me as a mother. I listened intently as it unfolded within me.

"Abby, everyone is running a race in this journey called life. Picture yourself on a track running the race I have called you to run. Do you see yourself running around the track? Do you see the spectators in the stands, some cheering you on, but most of them are commenting in some negative way about the way you are running your race with your son? Every single person has spectators as they run their own race in life. What is happening right now within you is that you are listening too much to the negative spectators. You care too much about how people view you as a mother and how they view Shia as your son. You feel as if you need to explain to everyone why you are doing what you are doing and why Shia is the way he is. You are trying to make them understand why you are running the way you are running. Stop doing that! What you do in that very moment is you stop running the race completely to go up to the stands to talk to these negative spectators. Do you see the danger in this? You will always have people in your life that have something negative to say about your race. Their purpose is only to distract you, to cause you to stumble, to make you feel like a failure and bring feelings of insecurity, to make you feel defeated and weak, to cause you to fear and doubt, to make you feel frustrated, even angry at times, and ultimately to take your focus off the race. I have called you to run. I want you to ignore them and keep running! Or if you must, give them a shout-out as you run past them that lets them know you are not concerned or affected by their opinions or thoughts, and then just keep running. The only power they have is the power you give them. When you focus on them, you are giving them your power."

As I sat in that moment of stillness pondering these thoughts, I felt more guidance coming from that still small voice.

"You also often struggle with comparing yourself to others and comparing Shia to other children. Again, picture yourself running on that track. You are running the way I have called you to run. Right? There are times you feel completely confident in how you are running the race as a mother and how Shia is running his very own race, but then something happens. Instead of staying focused on your race, you find yourself looking at the person running next to you. You become so focused on how they are running and how their kids are running that you completely lose all motivation to keep running the race I have set you and Shia on.

You wonder what is wrong with you? What is wrong with Shia? You think your race isn't fair and you long to be running their race. You become so insecure that you start trying to run the way they run, thinking that will make you and Shia better. What happens when you have thoughts like this is you switch lanes and get in theirs, and you pick up Shia and put him in a different lane as well. Do you see the danger in this? I didn't call you or Shia to those races. I didn't equip you for someone else's race. I equipped you for yours, and I equipped Shia for his.

Comparing your race to others is just as bad as focusing on the negative spectators. It is very unwise to compare because it will cause you to become distracted. You will stumble and feel like a failure. You will become weak and weary. You will be filled with doubt, insecurity, and fear. You will become frustrated and angry, and you will ultimately stop running the race I have set before you. Do not do this! Stay focused on the race...your race...Shia's race. It is unfair to Shia to compare him to others. It is unfair to you to compare yourself to others. I have fearfully and wonderfully created both of you for a unique purpose—for your very own race. Run the race I have set before you. And know that I will provide everything you need to run the race victoriously."

Wow! What an eye-opener. Boy, did I need to hear that. That guidance was so powerful that I felt an immediate shift in my heart to start doing life differently. I felt encouraged to run my race that God had called me to run. However, not knowing anyone, I felt alone and isolated in Hawaii. I knew God was with me, but I just wanted to meet someone who had some sort of experience with children like Shia.

Giving Me Support

I had prayed and asked God to send me someone that had experience with children like Shia. Shortly after that prayer, we were at the park when a lady approached and introduced herself. She was drawn to talk to me, and she interacted with Shia beautifully. We had a wonderful conversation.

God clearly sent this amazing woman, Valerie, who had worked with special needs children for many years. That day she said she felt led to come to that park instead of going home. God had answered my prayers and brought me Valerie, who had much experience with children like Shia. We soon became good friends. Later she told me that on that day we met, God had whispered to her to just love on us. We are still friends today. Later in the story, I will share more about her.

Chapter 9

HEALTH CHALLENGES

Spring 2014: Not Feeling Myself

I was feeling off and not feeling like myself. The Army provides medical insurance as part of their military benefits, so I decided to see my primary care doctor. He ran tests and everything came back normal, which was reassuring. With all the new changes in my life and with the intensity of everything, my doctor assumed it was from stress. At that time, I thought it was probably stress as well. So, I left and continued my journey just feeling off. It would be one more challenge that I would learn to stand up against and not let it steal my peace.

Chase Down Your Blessing

Shia and I went for a walk and ended at a park to play. As he was playing, my eyes were drawn to a particular mom who had her newborn tucked closely to her chest and wrapped in a swaddle carrier. Yet she was playing and interacting with her young son. I am not much of a people watcher, but I am open to being led by the Spirit to move as He moves me. My eyes kept noticing how patient, attentive, loving, and encouraging she was with her children.

A short time later I felt it was time to leave, so I packed our things and noticed that the mother was also preparing to leave. Shia and I began to leave in a different direction from the mother when God spoke to my heart and said, "Go to her. Tell her what you think of her as a mother. Tell her what I showed you." Naturally, I turned around and went in the other direction after her. By that time, she was at least a couple of blocks ahead of me, so I picked up the pace.

I stopped at the crosswalk stop light, putting us even further behind. I thought, *Never mind; I've missed the opportunity.* So, I started my walk back home in the other direction. After about 20 feet of walking, the Spirit nudged me again and said, "She needs encouragement. Go to her." In obedience, I took off running after her. Shia was giggling as he loves to go fast in the stroller. It was then that she turned around and noticed us.

I thought she would probably think I was a crazy woman, as I yelled after her. She stopped, and I caught up to her. I then asked her if we could walk with her for a bit. Then I proceeded to tell her that I was watching her at the park and that I thought she was a wonderful, attentive, and encouraging mother, which is rare to see. I could tell she was blessed by just those few words as her face revealed her effort to hold back tears.

We walked and I quickly learned her name was Rae. After 20 or more minutes of sharing life experiences with one another, I walked away so blessed. She later revealed that on that morning she had been having a rough start of the day and was deeply blessed and encouraged by the "crazy lady" who ran after her to tell her she was a great mother.

The biggest surprise was learning that she was also a mother of a special needs, nonverbal child. God had provided me that much needed support. I was blessed to have a new friend in Rae with whom we could both share our unique life experiences. From that first meeting, we quickly became close friends and frequently met at parks to talk and share our experiences.

God's plans are always perfect. Meeting Rae in the park that day brought another blessing. Rae, her husband, and children were a military family. Like us, they had decided to move off post, and without knowing where we lived, they moved to our complex. There are no coincidences with God.

One day Rae and her sons were visiting with us, and Rae said that her one son was autistic. I told her that I didn't think he was. It was almost like I was trying to convince her of something that she had already come to grips with and had fully embraced her

69

son's diagnosis. There was something about the word autistic, autism, and labeling a child with a diagnosis that I continued to resist.

They Are Just Words

Tim and I had suspected that Shia was autistic, but I struggled greatly with getting a diagnosis because I didn't want Shia to wear a label for his entire life. I was learning to accept the path that God had called me to follow, while embracing Shia for who he was. Putting a label on him was an entirely different level of acceptance. I did NOT want people identifying Shia as anything other than Shia.

My friend, Valerie, called me one day and asked if she could come for a visit. When she arrived, she eagerly began sharing something that God had shown her. "Yesterday, I woke up sobbing because of this revelation God gave me about you. It was powerful and so overwhelming."

I was intrigued. She continued, "You were sitting in the corner of your couch with your feet up and your arms were wrapped around your knees. You had your face buried in your knees. I saw all these words swirling around your head, and some were even attacking you — like hitting you on the shoulder and arms. Words like autistic, special needs, label, autism. You started crying, even sobbing, as the words kept coming at you. I can't really remember, but I feel like you were saying stop. I remember it was very dark, and the words were white like smoke. And I heard God's voice, 'They're just words. They can't hurt you. Shia will still be the same. They don't change him.' And then specifically, I heard Him say to me in a louder voice, 'Tell her to stop fearing words.'"

Hearing her words from God was a breakthrough moment for me because just the night before I was sharing my concerns and hesitancy with my husband about getting Shia diagnosed. I did not want to label him. Tim firmly told me, "Abby, they are just words. They don't have any power unless we give them power." Valerie sharing the revelation that God had given was a deep confirmation to move forward with getting Shia diagnosed.

A Mom at Target

My little Shia is such an explorer. He has been this way since he could crawl, and Tim and I have always allowed him to explore and learn no matter the location. In saying that, when we go out in public, we tend to get those looks. I can only imagine what people are thinking, where as it does not bother Tim one bit. However, in past experiences, I have allowed it to eat at me...worrying about other people's opinions, which would often lead me to removing Shia from certain places or telling him to stop what he was doing.

One day, while at Target, I was watching a mother who had two children who were exploring, laughing, and having a great time. They weren't being crazy or rude or destroying the store, just having fun exploring. I wasn't judging her. I was admiring the family and relieved to see this taking place. She caught me looking at her and immediately told her children, "Okay, that is enough playing. Settle down."

That moment, God showed me how I looked when I worried about what other people were thinking as they watched Shia having his own form of fun. I was moved to say something to this mom...something I might have liked to have heard if the situation had been reversed.

I approached that mother and said, "I am so glad you let your children explore in the store." She was completely thrown off by my comment and said, "I always wonder what the other parents are thinking." I replied, "I am often intimidated by other people as well because I also have a little explorer. So, it is nice to see you allowing your children to explore and have a good time."

I could tell she was surprised by my comments and most likely had experienced dirty looks and possibly negative comments. But I am confident she had never had anyone thank her for allowing her children to noisily explore and enjoy life. I walked away smiling, believing she felt encouraged.

As we left Target, I silently thanked God for blessing me with my amazing, exploring Shia. I could tell God was using Shia to help free me from caring about what other people thought of me as a mom. My great desire was to become more like my amazing and confident husband, Tim, who was able to move through life and not give a rip about what other people thought of Shia or of me as a mom.

Special Needs Doctor

As I continued to run my race, God brought me another friend with a special needs child. Beth was a member of a Facebook group for late talkers, as was I. She read my post in which I mentioned living in Hawaii. She was also living in Hawaii and wanted to reach out to me.

We agreed to meet at a park where we chatted and connected beautifully. Shortly after our initial meeting, we bumped into each other at the local coffee shop and started talking. Both of us had been researching the same special needs naturopathic doctor in the area. I was intrigued and felt God saying this was my next step, so I contacted the doctor and booked an appointment for Shia.

While at the appointment, I saw a picture on the wall of a swimmer diving into the ocean. Printed on the picture was one word—TRUST. I felt at that moment, God was telling me to trust Him as we would dive into this journey…together. "I am right here with you. I have your hand. Though you may stumble, you will not fall. I've got you. Trust Me."

We still had not gotten Shia tested at this point. This appointment was the first time I saw the word autism written on paperwork in relation to Shia. I am so thankful God gave my friend Valerie the revelation she shared with me and that God had spoken through my husband about autism being just a word without any power to define Shia as a person. It gave me something to stand on as God walked me through it all.

The only power that words have is the power I give them. It was my choice to either allow words to rob my peace or ignore those words. I was reminded that Shia was fearfully and wonderfully made just the way he is. The word "autism" did not change that truth.

It took a bit to find my footing as we stepped into the official diagnoses, but even though I stumbled, God was faithfully walking hand in hand and guiding me through it all. Shia was officially diagnosed with severe to moderate autism, severe receptive/ expressive language disorder, and sensory processing disorder.

Diet and Supplements for Shia

I knew God led me to this naturopathic doctor, and I was preparing to do all that she asked of me to help Shia better cope with the symptoms of autism. At that time in our lives, Shia rarely was sleeping through the night. He also seemed to have some digestive issues along with being an extremely picky eater.

The doctor wanted to get blood work done, plus urine and stool samples. She also advised that we make some changes to his diet and give him her recommended supplements. I was overwhelmed by it all and wondered how in the world I would be able to get Shia to cooperate. The doctor was very empathetic to our situation and offered encouragement.

I remember crying out to God that night with overwhelming emotions, and He reminded me to just dive in and trust that He would faithfully guide me as He always had. I had to take a lot of time to put into practice my training of being still. Be still; let go; trust God; and listen to His still small voice. God always showed up time and time again and spoke His directions to me.

The homeopathic drops tasted awful, and it was literally just a few small drops. God spoke to me and told me to squirt the drops into his mouth after he fell asleep. It worked brilliantly, so I mixed another nasty tasting supplement and put them into a big syringe. I then made it a game with lots and lots of tickles and squirted it in his mouth and chased it with water. Again, it worked brilliantly.

With all the new diet changes, I was convinced Shia would push back and refuse when I introduced something new...like switching from dairy to a nondairy product and adding good fats like avocado to his burrito or switching to all gluten-free products. By letting go and seeking God's guidance, I was able to slowly introduce these foods that were new to him. That often required mixing the old with a little bit of the new food and each day mixing just a little more of the new to gradually replace the old. Additionally, there needed to be a gradual introduction of a very small amount of good fats by adding a bit more each day. It too worked brilliantly. As I dove into this new regimen and trusting God to guide me in making these changes, Shia's sleep improved dramatically, which was a beautiful blessing to all of us.

Blood Work

The night before Shia's appointment for his first blood draw, I was deeply concerned about Shia's possible response. To make it even harder, Tim could not be with us.

I remember praying and asking God to allow me to see Him powerfully work the next day. I hoped for a private room because I felt in my heart that Shia would struggle. He had never had a needle stuck in him. With the severe expressive/receptive language disorder, this would make it very difficult and confusing for Shia to understand what was about to take place. I knew we most likely would need to pin him down to get this done, and this made me so sad. I wanted to be strong and peaceful for Shia. It would take all my courage to step into this with him.

The next day we arrived at the appointment, and as I was checking in Shia, I shared my concerns and details about him being autistic, nonverbal, and not being able to understand things. A lady, who was standing behind the front desk had overheard me talking and was moved with great compassion. She immediately came over and said to follow her. Much to my surprise, she took us to a private room and showed us great kindness and patience. Another lady assisted, but as they began the process of taking Shia's blood, it didn't go well the first time. Shia was kicking, crying, and resisting. He was angry and scared, and I asked if we could just stop. I held Shia and began singing the first song that came to my heart, thinking it would calm him down. The song was "Thy Word" by Amy Grant. To my surprise, the lady, who had offered the private room, said softly, "That is my favorite song." Then she began singing with us.

Unfortunately, our singing didn't help calm down Shia, so we stopped singing, and I continued holding Shia while he was upset. The lady who joined me in singing asked, "Mom, are you okay?" I looked up at her with tears in my eyes and said nothing. She immediately stopped everything and with no hesitation said, "Let's pray."

I was somewhat surprised, wondering if people really do this for strangers...especially in a public workplace? Both ladies prayed and laid their hands on Shia. Tears were flowing from my eyes. The other ladies were tearing up as well as the atmosphere completely changed, and Shia melted into my arms, overtaken by peace. I felt the Presence of God so powerfully. We were able to get the blood drawn on the second attempt and afterward, we sat for a while and visited while Shia enjoyed his snacks and toys.

I shared that I had prayed the night before and through them, my prayer was answered beyond my expectations. I thanked them for their patience and kindness towards Shia and me. We all talked a little more about the faithfulness of God. It was such a sweet moment. And to top off this appointment, the lady who sang with me and who had called us to pray, said with tears in her eyes, "I am never in the front, but for some reason, I felt led to go to the front at the exact moment you arrived." She went on to share, "I needed this today. I needed to see God work." Tears continued to fall as I pondered God's faithfulness in that moment. Because I trusted Him, He had powerfully shown up and answered my prayer.

Encouraging a Mom

I was laying out by the pool while Tim and Shia were inside the condo. Everyone who was at the pool left shortly after I arrived, and for about 20 minutes, I sat alone, enjoying the peace and quiet and being still. Then a small group of people with a little baby arrived. The baby was crying and the mother and several of her friends were trying to calm the infant down. After several minutes, I overheard the mom say, "I bet this lady over here hates me." Clearly, she was talking about me because I was the only other lady there.

I couldn't help but smile, knowing in the past I had also had similar thoughts and worries about what other people were thinking. A little while later I felt led to get up and encourage this mother. I walked over to her, patted her on the back, smiled, and said, "I don't hate you." You could tell she was relieved. I continued, "I get it. I have a little one, and it has taken me almost four years not to worry about what other people are thinking about me as a mother or about my child, Shia. I know I am doing the best job I can, and it looks like you are too. It is not like you are neglecting your child. You are trying to calm her. My husband has taught me that if I am doing the very best I can, everyone else can stick it. Don't focus on others. You're doing a great job." After we shared a little more, I walked away leaving her smiling and encouraged.

Services For Shia

Shia's naturopathic doctor shared with us that because we were military and had great insurance coverage, a large door for support would be opened for Shia for his therapies. But the evaluation and diagnosis would need to come from the military pediatric development doctor. I hadn't yet thought about therapies. I didn't know where to start with it all, but I was blessed and grateful to know they would be completely covered.

The journey had just begun with the full realization of having a child with special needs, but I kept letting go and trusting God to give me the grace to be Shia's mother. It was a process for me to find deep peace.

All healing is a process. Every layer God revealed to me took a bit to process and heal, but as I kept relying on my training and seeking God with all my heart, I felt Him walking hand in hand with me.

Chapter 10

GOD IS IN
THE STRUGGLES

Spring 2015: Still Not Myself

I was still not feeling like myself. Maybe it was just anxiety symptoms. I was very familiar with those symptoms from my past, but something felt different about what I was experiencing. I went back to the doctor and they ran more tests. Even though they all came back normal, I wasn't convinced that all was normal. Fortunately, I had an amazing doctor who answered all my questions and listened to my concerns, which led to his decision to dive a bit deeper with an EKG. The results were normal, so he went even deeper and ordered an echocardiogram.

A short time later, I had my first echocardiogram. I wasn't really expecting them to find anything because I wasn't having any major symptoms. My blood pressure was normal, my EKG was normal, my oxygen level was normal, and all my blood work was normal.

The echocardiogram took about 45 minutes. The tech dimmed the lights low so I could relax. I was lying comfortably and enjoying the quiet when I distinctly heard the still small voice say,

"You know I am always with you, right?" To which I thought, *Yes of course.* I continued to enjoy the peace, calm, and stillness. Then, suddenly everything changed in a moment.

The technician said, "I need to go get a cardiologist right now!" He then left me alone in a dark room. I had no idea what was going on and was quickly overtaken by intense fear. My heart was racing, I was shaking, and my palms were sweating. I then understood why God reassured me that He was always with me.

The cardiologist arrived and said, "You have a very large amount of fluid around your heart, and we need to figure out why." She then proceeded to ask me questions about symptoms to which I had none. I told her that I ran two miles several times a week with no issues. I then asked the possible cause of the fluid. She answered that it could be cancer, an autoimmune disorder, some sort of virus, or caused by many other things. She then said, "I am going to order some tests. We will also need to keep an eye on the fluid, which would require coming in for regular echocardiograms."

I left that office in a complete daze and overtaken by fear. On the drive home, I was fearing all the medical possibilities, so I immediately called my mom, but she didn't answer. As I continued driving in silence and processing my thoughts and emotions, I heard God say, "I need you to not tell your mom what is going on, because you know she will be on the first plane to Hawaii to be with you. I am going deeper into your heart, and I need you to put your comfort in Me being with you and not your mom."

When I got home, I shared all the details with my husband, but he seemed totally unconcerned. He confidently said, "You're fine. You don't have any of those things. This is just your test." He went on to say, "You have such a tight grip on your health, thinking that you are fully in control of it, but you are just going to have to let go and walk this out." I wanted to anchor into those words, but I didn't have the depth of trust at that time. But God was about to tend to the deeper matters of my heart.

I am a very health-conscience person, so I struggled with Shia's health. I thought I was doing everything right, and yet autism still surfaced. I had the same feelings about myself. I put into practice everything I shared in my book, *Living Still,* in regards to taking care of your body. I was taking good care of myself and doing everything I was supposed to do....so why was this happening? Tim was right. I did have a tight grip. It is wise to take care of your health but believing that you are in full control of the outcome is unrealistic. That was where I needed to let go and trust God with my life.

Shortly after our conversation, I sat crying and praying on our bed. I said, "God, obviously, there is still a fear deeply rooted in me. I had been completely peaceful, but this report has caused me to lose all my footing in You. Fear has overtaken me. Do whatever You need to do to remove this fear from me." I went on to pray,

"God, I don't want to be tossed by the storms. Despite what I am going through, I want people to see me steady, stable, and fully rooted in You."

God frequently speaks to me through my beautiful Shia and his love for nature. These pictures captured his fearlessness as he stood balanced, steady, courageous, stable, and firmly planted. This was God's message to me to be fearless, courageous, steady, stable, and firmly planted in Him as I walked this out.

I felt hard-pressed on every side with all that was going on in my life. Tim was preparing to be away for some training, which would leave me alone on this journey with Shia. But God reminded me often that He was with me, walking hand in hand with me. He was teaching that my security was not in Tim or my mom being with me. My security had to be in God and Him alone.

During this season in my life, I was having a hard time falling asleep. My mind would be filled with so many thoughts, that I had to rely on my training to take my thoughts captive. One night while lying in bed, I felt led to read this verse that powerfully spoke to me, "You will keep him in perfect peace those whose mind is stayed on you, because he trusts in you" (Isaiah 26:3 ESV). I then personalized the verse to read, "You will keep *me* in perfect peace because *my* mind stays on You, because *I* trust You." I whispered this every night over and over and over. It helped me to keep my mind focused on the truth in God's Word and to fall asleep.

Test After Test

Over the next year, I underwent numerous tests that included blood work, echocardiograms, heart monitors, stress tests, chest x-rays, mammograms, urine samples, stool samples, and several different ultrasounds and other testing. Thankfully, military insurance paid for everything. God was providing for our needs.

Each time I was required to have another test, fear surfaced that required God to tend to that fear and till those deep-rooted areas that cause me to struggle. It wasn't fun, but I courageously embraced it all with His help. I wanted to be set free from all that wasn't of God.

I leaned heavily on God to carry me through this trial. I relied fully on my training to rest in God as I faced each test head-on with Him. A deepening trust was developing in God as I courageously stepped up to the plate, embraced it, and learned from it.

Questions kept resurfacing as I was learning to dive deeper and deeper into trusting God: "Did I truly trust God with my life?" "Did I truly trust His plans?" "Did I truly believe that He was sovereign and in control and that my time on this earth was completely in His hands?"

Tim Struggles

I am so grateful Tim was rock-steady in those areas where I was deeply struggling. He was exactly what I needed him to be to keep moving forward. I couldn't imagine me trying to deal with everything and then have him feeling like he was drowning as well. That would have been even more difficult for both of us. But Tim was struggling intensely with many other things, yet he would not talk about them with me.

During that time of Tim's struggling, I felt closed off from him. We needed each other, but we were both dealing with so many things. He wasn't any source of encouragement or comfort, nor was he open for me to be any source of comfort or encouragement for him. This was incredibly difficult to endure.

I remember night after night, for what seemed like the longest time, Tim would come home so incredibly weighted and stressed by what was going on at work and everything else he was internalizing, that it began to take a toll on him. He became a very unpleasant person to live with most of the time, and I remember telling him, "I love you, but I don't like you right now."

The way Tim was choosing to deal with his own refiner's fire affected the atmosphere in our home. It became so intense at times that, instead of relying on my training, I was often tempted to give up, pack my bags, and take Shia with me to Missouri. In those moments, everything in me just wanted to run away from it all. When I would have these thoughts, God would speak to me and say, "Going home would be the easy route. That is not the route I have called you to take." It was a very intense spiritual workout, and it took a great deal for me to press into God and be able to persevere in the middle of everything that was happening and not give up on our marriage. Though I felt hard-pressed on every side,

I knew deep down I was not crushed, and that God was walking each day with me (2 Corinthians 4:8).

Trust in the Lord with All Your Heart

All the tests they ran were like the previously mentioned spiritual workout designed to build my trust muscles. God showed up in many ways to encourage me during those months of testing.

One proverb kept crossing my path, "Trust in the Lord with all your heart and lean not on your own understanding; in all your ways acknowledge Him and He will direct your path" (Proverbs 3:5-6 NKJV). Having a degree in health and wellness and other health-related certifications, it became challenging not to lean on my own understanding. Ironically, time and time again, this verse kept showing up.

During this time, I had some friends and a couple of family members faithfully praying for me and offering words of encouragement. The following text messages show how God was encouraging my heart. The first text came from my brother-in-law, James.

James – "This was the verse I wrote on Lori's Love note this morning... I was sort of stressed for time and almost skipped writing her a note at all, but I felt a beckon to sit down and read and pray over this verse... I pray that it means as much to you as it did to me this morning. 'Trust in the Lord with all your heart and lean not on your own understanding; in all your ways submit to him, and he will make your paths straight' (Proverbs 3:5-6 NIV). Is your path straight? In all your ways, submit to him! Love you, Abby! Love you to my core! "

I was so overjoyed with the encouragement that I shared the news with my dear friends Matt and Becca. I texted them what James had sent to me. The following was Matt's reply and our conversation back and forth.

Matt – "Amen! That was the verse this Sunday in our home sermon :) Had a dream last week that a big black man came up to me and hugged me crying like we were brothers and then said that verse to me and I woke up ;)

Abby – "Really? The man that did my first echocardiogram, which revealed all of this, was a big black man. I am sure I will see him again through all of this. Interesting."

The encouragement continued as I shared these above text messages with my cousin Kendra and her husband, Nelson, who were also praying for me. This is what Kendra texted me.

Kendra – "I have to tell you this. Nelson has been praying, and he got up and went outside. He brought his Bible in from the car. I said, let me read what Abby just sent me. I saw a tear and then he took a labored breath and started bawling. He finally got it out and said, that's the verse I was looking up to send to Abby!! He is still bawling."

Kendra shared further in her text message, "Now, since yesterday, that scripture had been stirring my spirit, and I was going to send it to you, but the Holy Spirit stopped me and said not now!!"

Truly powerful. What a jolt!!! God had my attention. I was locked in and focused more now because of that amazing encouragement that He gave me through my friends and family.

A short time later, I went to Rae's house, so the kids could play, and we could visit. A new picture with scripture verses was hanging on the wall of her condo, and to my surprise, Proverbs 3:5-6 was printed on the picture. They were the exact verses that God, friends, and family had shared with me. Rae did not know the significance of those scriptures in my life, but when I commented about the picture, she gave it to me! She said that the kids kept knocking it off the wall.

Rae had no idea how much that gift blessed me. That cherished picture immediately was hung on the wall in our Hawaii condo. Later it found its home on the wall of my Be Love Give Love office. It would always serve as a reminder of God's faithfulness in walking hand in hand throughout all areas of my life and knowing that I could fully trust Him.

You Are Not Alone

I remember the day when I felt led to go for a run. My cardiologist had given me the okay to continue running because the fluid was not affecting my physical health, and my heart was functioning completely normal despite the large amount of fluid. At this point, she had mentioned that I might have been born with this anomaly, making it normal for me, which gave me a sense of comfort.

While running, I wanted to shrink back in fear and stop running. What if something happened? But God told me, "Press into Me, trust Me, and keep running. You are not alone in this. I am right here with you."

I kept running, and it was during that time that God brought me the song, "I Am Not Alone" by Kari Jobe, which spoke powerfully to my heart. I listened to it on repeat when running, and with God, I courageously faced those deep-rooted fears. The lyrics reminded me that no matter the trials, the battles, or the fires of adversity, God was always with me. Even in deepest sorrow, I was not alone, because He was with me. He was my strength and defender, and that life-giving truth resonated deep within my heart and soul. ("I Am Not Alone" can be listened to on YouTube.)

Each time I listened to that song, I intensely felt God's Presence and knew that He had me in the shadow of His wings, just like that special day when He spoke to me as I stood under the umbrella tree. I was encouraged deeply and reassured that He was walking with me.

Going to Bed Angry

During this intense season with Tim, God began to take me deeper into truth regarding the dangers of having strife in our home and going to bed angry. I was listening to a sermon online, and the pastor focused on James 3:16 that says where there is strife, there is *every* evil work. That word *every* stood out to me. He then said, "Do everything you can to get rid of *all* strife in your home, because if you don't, you are basically giving Satan an open door to bring in *every* evil work." That got my attention.

I felt led to look deeper, so I looked up the definition of "strife" and found that strife is defined as "angry or bitter disagreement." Other names for strife are conflict, discord, dispute, friction, argument, and quarreling. I then read, "Be angry and do not sin; do not let the sun go down on your anger and give no opportunity to the devil" (Ephesians 4:26-27 ESV). This gave me a deeper understanding of why it was so important not to allow anger and bitterness in our marriage.

Thankfully, prior to this season, Tim and I had gotten rid of destructive behaviors such as giving the cold shoulder, silent treatments, sleeping in the other room, withholding our love from each other, having a spirit of division in our home or in our hearts towards each other, or going to bed angry. During that intense refiner's fire season, those things were starting to resurface and creep back into our marriage.

I told Tim what God was revealing to me about strife, but I am not sure it took root in his heart or if he even heard me, because I was the one who had to push back against the weight of the strife and encourage him to talk things out and to have the hard conversations before going to bed. As difficult as it was, we would stay up late having those difficult conversations for as long as needed. Unfortunately, we didn't go to bed with our problems resolved because Tim would not share what he was struggling with internally. However, we always forgave each other, so the air was light and clear and with no division in our hearts before going to sleep.

There were many late nights of staying up late to clear the air. I became so frustrated with Tim because he was never the first to suggest our need to talk. I was also mad and didn't always want to talk it through.

I struggled with myself always being what I thought was the "bigger person" and doing the right thing. I remember wrestling with this and asking God why I was always the first one to say that we needed to clear the air? Why isn't Tim saying anything? Isn't he the leader of our home and family? Doesn't he understand the danger? Why isn't he standing up against this?

God whispered something so powerful to me that it immediately shifted my heart. He said, "You are more sensitive. You can sense the intensity of it before Tim does. Don't worry about who is doing what with this matter. Just be grateful someone is sensing it and standing up against Satan. Remember your battle is not with Tim; it is with the powers of darkness" (Ephesians 6:12). From then on, I knew the position God put me in, and I was grateful for being able to sense the presence of darkness in our home and take a stand against it, even though it required me to take the initiative.

Chapter 11

TRUSTING GOD

Fall 2015: Shift in Focus

Shia's fifth birthday arrived, and I was up before everyone. I was sitting alone in the quiet with my thoughts, focusing on all the things Shia lacked and how he should have been further along in his development. At that time, Shia still had very limited speech. At age five he had not yet said, "I love you, Mommy." I desperately wanted to hear him speak his thoughts, wants, desires, needs, and what was going on in his little mind. As I kept thinking about all the things Shia lacked and all the things he was missing in his life, I became very sad and a sudden thought interrupted me: *I would hate it if someone focused on all those things they thought I lacked as a woman in this world.*

Shia is an amazing child—unique and different—but so amazing. God showed me that morning that I was forgetting all the things Shia did *not* lack and forgetting all the things I loved about him. I continued to sit with my thoughts and my heavy heart, and then through tears, I prayed and asked God to encourage my heart as Shia's mother.

A few moments later, I felt led to write all the things I loved about Shia. After the first five things, the heaviness starting to lift.

So, I continued writing about everything I love about Shia and how truly grateful I am for him just as he is. I wrote the following words on the morning of his fifth birthday:

I love his pace in life.

I love that he is never in a hurry.

I love that he stops to take life in fully.

I love how he slows me down even more in life.

I love his love for stillness.

I love that he is an explorer at heart.

I love his carefree spirit.

I love that he doesn't care what other people think about him.

I love his quiet nature.

I love his simplicity.

I love his independence.

I love his natural leadership qualities.

I love his passion when he is focused on something he enjoys.

I love his laugh.

I love his kisses.

I love his hugs.

I love his fearlessness.

I love his courage.

I love his love for trees.

I love that he loves to be outside.

I love that he loves to be barefoot.

I love his love for building forts and obstacle courses.

I love his love for learning.

I love his love for music.

I love that he is not a follower.

I love his sensitivity to the Spirit.

I love how God has used him to teach me so much.

After completing my list, I sat with it and read and reread it. As tears streamed down my face, and with a deep joy in my heart, I felt truly blessed to have Shia for my son. My prayer was answered. I felt deeply encouraged as God led me to shift my focus to all the great qualities and things I loved about my son. Though nothing about my son changed that day, my perspective, my mindset, and my attitude changed, which allowed me to walk in deeper peace and joy.

Test Results

Thankfully all the tests came back normal, and my cardiologist said she had exhausted all testing except for a pericardial tap. I asked what that was, and she proceeded to tell me that I would be sedated. They would then stick a large needle into the sack around my heart to extract some fluid and have it sent for testing. I asked about the potential danger, and she assured me that it had been done many times with zero complications. I agreed to having the procedure, but then she said there is always a chance that my heart would not like "messing with the fluid." Of course, that isn't something I wanted to hear, so once again, fear surfaced with the "what-ifs." Despite this, I had a knowing that it was the next step, and I courageously agreed to have it done.

I Am Weary, God

At this point, I was weary with life. There were the uncertainties of my future, Shia's future, and Tim's future with military life and deployments. Once again, fear surfaced in my heart. I needed comfort. So where could I run? I ran to my God, my loving Father in Heaven. I chose to be still and ask Him to lead me to verses that would comfort me. I was searching, with all my heart, for hidden treasure within God's Word, I knew God would speak to me through His word if I would remain in that "place of stillness" until I found it. The following are the two verses (treasures) that spoke directly to my heart.

"Peace, I leave with you; My [own] peace I now give and bequeath to you. Not as the world gives do I give to you. Do not let your hearts be troubled, neither let them be afraid. [Stop allowing yourselves to be agitated and disturbed; and do not permit yourselves to be fearful and intimidated and cowardly and unsettled."] (John 14:27 AMPC)

"The person who has My commands and keeps them is the one who [really] loves Me; and whoever [really] loves Me will be loved by My Father, and I [too] will love him and will show (reveal, manifest) Myself to him. [I will let Myself be clearly seen by him and make Myself real to him.]" (John 14:21 AMPC)

After pondering these scriptures, especially the second verse, I asked God to please reveal and manifest Himself to me that day.

Four hours later, while on a walk and enjoying God's beautiful creation with Shia, I captured this photo with the heart in the sky.

God has used hearts to speak directly to me. I believe that He does it to remind me of His great love for me and that He is always with me, guiding and directing my life. This moment deeply touched me and gave me that jolt I need to keep moving forward.

Push Myself

The day arrived for the pericardial tap procedure. I was anxious, so I reached out to a dear friend for prayer. She wrote, "I know God is working right now. I woke about an hour and a half ago. In my sleep, you were in my thoughts. Almost as if your name was being whispered in my ear, I started praying for you, asking God to be with you, wrapping you in His gentle arms, and comforting you. I continued to pray until I got out of bed and that is when I looked at my phone in the kitchen and saw your text. My resounding prayer was centered around this scripture, 'Be strong and courageous, do not be afraid, do not be discouraged, for the Lord God is with you wherever you go' (Joshua 1:9 NIV). Press into Him, do not let your anxious thoughts turn your eyes away from God's Light! Step out of that sticky tar. Let the light of Jesus clean you off. I am continuing to pray for you, Abby!"

The day I arrived at the hospital I was walking on the sidewalk into the hospital when I noticed a person wearing a shirt that read on the back "Loads of Hope." God whispered, "Stay hopeful, Abby." Then, when getting into the elevator, the person standing in front of me was wearing a shirt that read, "Push Yourself." I was immediately jolted by God with courage and strength. Then, if that wasn't enough, the resident doctor on duty was named Faith, and God whispered, "Have faith. I am here, walking this out hand in hand with you."

Clean Bill of Health

The tests came back normal with a clean bill of health. Although the test was normal, the cardiologist felt it was wise to continue monitoring the fluid. I told her that we would be changing duty stations later in the year. She assured me that I only needed to get established with a cardiologist at the new location. She then released me and said, "Go and live your life normally." I was peaceful. All seem well and good. I felt free. It was all over.

I didn't think much about the fluid, except when I had to get my routine echocardiograms, which showed my heart was functioning perfectly, despite having close to a liter of fluid around it. Interestingly, the heart is only supposed to have 10-50 ml in the sac around your heart. Mine was holding 800-1000 ml.

We enjoyed the rest of our time in Hawaii, living life with this new freedom, and then we relocated to North Carolina.

Chapter 12

OPPORTUNITIES TO GROW

Summer 2016: Getting Established in North Carolina

Upon arriving and getting settled into North Carolina, the anxious process began of getting Shia evaluated and officially diagnosed through the military pediatric development doctor. I felt God with me every step of the way as we ventured into this next chapter of our lives.

We were blessed with a great pediatric development doctor. She was wonderful with Shia and offered a lot of helpful advice, encouragement, and resources for therapy. She put in all our referrals for speech, occupational, and Applied Behavior Analysis (ABA) therapy. Lots and lots of paperwork began the very long process of getting Shia evaluated for each therapy. The process had not been started in Hawaii, due to all the things that surfaced regarding the issue with the heart fluid. Plus, we knew we would be leaving Hawaii soon, so Tim and I thought it would be best to get services started for Shia in North Carolina.

Shia's evaluator, Katie, was amazing with him for his Occupational Therapy (OT). She worked beautifully with him, and he seemed to really like her. Watching her interaction with Shia, caused me to hope that she could be his therapist. Then I felt the nudge to just ask, which she replied that she had no openings. Though disappointed, I chose to release it to God, knowing He would place him with the right person.

I tried to schedule our first OT appointment with a therapist, but the scheduler was not there. The next day I received a phone call from the scheduler, and once again, I felt a nudge to mention the wonderful therapist Shia had seen for his evaluation and how much we would love to have her work with him. To my surprise, she said that Katie just had a time slot open. Most amazing of all, was that the time slot worked perfectly for sessions to be back-to-back with the time we already made for Shia's scheduled speech session. This blessed me so much, and I whispered, "God, You are so faithful. This proves once again that You go before us and take care of everything we need as we trust and rely on You."

I got established with a new cardiologist and booked my first appointment. Little did I know that before my appointment, God would do more tugging and pulling on some things that were still deeply rooted in my heart. Thankfully, He is so gracious to take us through things little by little, step-by-step, because He knows what we are capable of handling.

Another Layer of Fear

My new cardiologist reviewed my entire patient file, all the test results, and all the echocardiograms. I was expecting to just pick up where we left off in Hawaii. In my mind, this was just more monitoring. But this cardiologist had an entirely different outlook on my situation than my previous cardiologist in Hawaii.

During that first appointment, he spoke some words over me that sent me into yet another intense refiner's season.

I felt grateful that over several months, I had not thought much about the heart fluid situation. God knows what He is doing as the Master Gardener. He gave me a much-needed break. But it was time to let Him do some more tilling of my "soil" to set me free. I did not want to fight against it, but this one was really tough.

My new cardiologist said, "You could die of sudden cardiac arrest! We need to get you well!" I trembled in fear as tears rolled down my cheeks, trying to process what he just spoke. I don't remember much more of the appointment after those words were spoken. The only thing I recall was coming out to the waiting room and seeing Shia and Tim. I immediately picked up Shia, hugged him tightly as I carried him outside and continued to cry while I held him in my arms.

So many thoughts flooded my mind. Tim had no idea what was going on as I had not yet shared the shocking news. After calming down a bit and getting Shia buckled in, we sat in the car as I told him what the cardiologist had said. I could tell this affected Tim differently than when I originally found out that I had fluid around my heart. This was huge. I was just told I could die at any moment from sudden cardiac arrest.

Tim then began to share with me about some upcoming training that would require him to be gone for a short time. He immediately said that he would not go and that he would try to get out of it. At first, I was relieved because I did not want to be alone, but then I sat there and felt God clearly say to me, "He must go." I then looked directly at Tim and with determination said, "You have to go. I need to walk this out with God. As hard as it might be, I can't fear being alone."

I knew this wouldn't be the only time in Tim's military career that would require him to be away from us. He couldn't stop doing what he was called to do just because of this news. After all, I had just gone through a mass amount of testing in Hawaii where my cardiologist told me to live my life. I had a deep knowing that all would be well and that this was just another area that God wanted to tend to in my heart so that roots of faith would continue to grow deeper and deeper in Him.

September 2016: My Birthday

My birthday was soon approaching, and I wanted something that spoke deeply to my heart to help me endure the season in which I was walking. We went shopping as a family for my birthday, and in a store, I saw a picture on the wall that powerfully struck me. I stood captivated by the picture and knew it had to go home with me. Tim bought it for me and hung it in our bedroom.

Each morning before getting out of bed, I would lie in bed and look at that picture and pray, "God let my faith be bigger than my fears today." Each day was a chance to choose to trust Him. Each day was a spiritual workout to grow roots deeper and deeper in God. This workout was intense, but I knew He was walking with me each step of the way.

Fall 2016: Starting Shia's Therapy

Shia started his different therapies, and I could feel God helping me let go of Shia and trust others to care for him and help him along his journey. God so graciously allowed me to start sessions of therapy with Shia, so I was able to be in the room with him. I wasn't yet ready to let go of my non-verbal child to be with a stranger.

Several things happened during Shia's sessions. First, I became aware of the tight grip I had and not trusting others with him. I needed to be in every session with Shia or have sessions in our home, so I could have some sense of control and see everything the therapist was doing. I wanted to protect Shia.

God had work to do in my heart because of the tight grip I had on Shia. It was hard for me to let go and trust others. But something else happened during these sessions. As I watched other professionals work with Shia, I felt like I was going through the therapy as well, because I was learning more about how to engage and interact with him.

Katie, our wonderful occupational therapist, taught me how to incorporate more breaks and countdowns with Shia. She could get Shia to do unpleasant tasks that I thought he would never do. She would have him do the activity once or for a brief time, and then he would get to take a fun break for about a minute doing an activity of his choosing. Then she would count down the ten remaining seconds left to play, and he would willingly return to the table to engage in the next task she presented. He knew the task wouldn't be too overwhelming and that it wasn't going to last a long time. Katie successfully did this time and time again, so I began applying those methods with great success in unpleasant task, such as brushing teeth, haircuts, and some homeschool activities that we were struggling with.

As I pondered Shia's progress, I went back to how much I resisted the diagnosis of autism. But by embracing the diagnosis and trusting God to walk with us in this journey, He had opened a door to so much support for both Shia and me.

106

God's faithfulness allowed me to trust in the people He had provided, so I began sitting in the waiting room while Shia had his session. Occasionally, I would join a session with them, so I could get my own refresher therapy session. To this day, Katie is still Shia's occupational therapist.

Voice of Truth

My cardiologist wanted to do some testing, which the cardiologist in Hawaii had not done. He ordered an MRI on my heart. This would show things that an echocardiogram would not show. Another test…another spiritual workout.

MRI's challenge you mentally. I had a past MRI regarding some intense back pain, so I was somewhat prepared. For those who have not had an MRI, you are confined in a very tight space for what seems an eternity...a completely uncomfortable experience, especially when trying not to think about what they might discover. God had told me to take my lavender eye pillow to place over my eyes to help me relax, which it did.

I had requested that they play Christian music while getting the test done, and God was once again there for me and said, "I am in this. I have you. You can trust me."

Years ago, when I had my first MRI, God encouraged me with a song, "Voice of Truth" by Casting Crowns, which played during the MRI imaging. That song allowed me to feel the Presence of God so intensely that tears of joy fell during the test.

This song had represented my heart's desire to have that kind of faith that trusts God so completely that I could step out of my comfort zone, into the unknown, and believe that God was with me.

In God's faithfulness and great love for me, He allowed that exact song to play during my heart MRI. Once again, I intensely felt God's Presence and was deeply encouraged to have the faith to climb out of the boat and onto the waves, knowing that Jesus was holding out His hand to me. Though the enemy of my soul told me, "You will never win," God's "voice of truth" told me over and over not to be afraid, because this was for God's glory. (You can listen to "Voice of Truth" on YouTube.)

The test came back, and everything was normal despite the fluid still being there. It seemed to pose no threat to me. The cardiologist was completely perplexed and said this was a very rare case. He had never seen anything like it. We continued doing regular echocardiograms to monitor me, but nothing changed.

Chapter 13

GOD PROVIDES

Early 2017: Buying a House

We were made aware that a majority of Tim's military career would more than likely have him stationed in North Carolina, so we felt we should invest in a home instead of renting. This would be our fourth move in four years. Talk about some intense letting go and flowing with the changes! We looked all over the area, but we were always led back to a certain area. We found a home that we both immediately had peace about. The backyard was what captured our hearts first, and Shia seemed to immediately enjoy it as well.

I searched the area for what was close to the home we were praying about, and when I zoomed out on the map, I discovered a park with walking trails and a small pond. It was about five minutes up the road from the house. My attention was quickly captured when I zoomed in on the pond, and to my surprise, the pond was in the shape of a heart.

Anderson Creek County Park

God continues to use hearts to speak to my heart as a reminder that He is walking hand in hand with me and my family. I felt that it was God nudging us in the direction of that home, so we moved forward with the purchase.

We Found a Church

Just a couple miles from our new home we found a church. As soon as I walked through the doors, there was a deep knowing that this was exactly where we were supposed to be. During the service, Shia was a bit unsettled because of the loud music, so Tim took him out to explore. A gentleman approached Tim to talk with him and quickly revealed that he also had an autistic child who was primarily nonverbal.

The following Sunday, Shia was again unsettled during the service, so this time, I took him outside of the sanctuary to explore. A lady approached to talk and engage with Shia. Not many people feel comfortable trying to interact with Shia, but this lady appeared to be a pro…and she was. Not only was she a mother of an autistic child, but she was also the site pastor's wife.

She shared information about the buddy program that the church offered for special needs children. The program allowed parents to enjoy the service together, while the children would be in another area of the church with a trained buddy. We were overwhelmed by God's provision, and immediately we got involved in the church, met new people, and enjoyed being a part of a church family.

Keep Pressing Forward

During this season, not only were the cardiologist's words, "You could die of sudden cardiac arrest," spoken over me several times, I was also told that I was a walking, ticking time bomb. At times, those words played loudly in my head, and it took pressing into God, day after day, hour after hour, minute after minute to find solid footing, peace, and stability. This was by far the hardest spiritual workout that I had ever endured at that point. But I knew God was walking with me and despite how intense this had become, I could and would trust Him.

I felt myself getting stronger in God with each passing day, but at times intense fear kept surfacing and completely taking over. I remember praying and asking God, "What is this fear that keeps surfacing? What is the root of why it keeps surfacing?" I felt God asking me to draw closer to Him. So, I fasted social media for a month to quiet all the outside noise. I knew God wanted me to dive deeper into this, and He needed my full attention.

I felt led to do a three-week Bible study on faith. As I went through this study, I got a revelation of the source of my fear when I heard God speak, "You are not afraid of dying. You have found deep peace with that. You know I have your days on this earth numbered, and you trust in My sovereignty and plan for your life, as well as Tim's and Shia's. But where this fear is coming from is you thinking that if you are no longer on this earth, who then will care for Shia the way you do because you know him better than anyone."

God went on to say, "Do you not think that if your time on earth is done, that I wouldn't have a plan for Shia as well? I love him more than you can imagine, and My plans for him are good as well. I need you to let go of him and trust Me. Don't fear. I will take care of Him if I call you back home to be with Me."

I cried and cried with this new revelation and prayed, "God, I know You are far more capable of taking care of Shia than I am. I let go of him. I trust in You." With this amazing revelation, I was able to let go of Shia and entrust him to God. I then felt God pull that fear out by the root, giving me a new sense of freedom.

Following this revelation, I felt strongly led to write a letter to Shia. I asked Tim to save it and that if God called me to be with Him, and my time on earth was complete, then I would like for him to read and re-read it to Shia. I didn't know if Shia would understand what I was saying in the letter, but it gave me a deeper peace knowing it was written and would be read if I wasn't here. The letter read:

My Beautiful Shia,

If you are reading this, then my journey on earth has come to an end. Earth is not our true home, son. We are spiritual beings having an earthly experience, and we each have a predestined time given by God, when our journey is over here on Earth. Even though we are apart on Earth, know that I am alive and well with Jesus.

You must trust that He knew best when he called me home. His plans are good even though they sometimes cause us great pain. I want you to stay focused on God and trust Him with all your heart. Do not try to understand why He allowed this to happen now in your life. Some things are left a mystery, but they test our faith and trust in God. Dig deeper into Him during this season. Allow God to use this to refine your faith and trust in Him. Don't lose faith. Don't lose trust. Never lose faith and trust in God. Stay close to Him always.

Take time to be still in God's Presence as often as you can...especially outside in nature. Keep your ears open to His still small voice as you journey through life. Be in this world, my son, but not of it. Stay true to your roots in God. Do not let the distractions and voices of this world cause you to stumble or to lose focus on what really matters, and that is our walk with God. Let the light and love of Christ shine brightly through you, Shia, greatly affecting the world around you.

You have a warrior spirit...strong, fearless, and courageous with a beautiful sensitivity to the Holy Spirit. Don't ever lose that. You are fearfully and wonderfully made by the loving hands of God. You are my special unique gift from God. You have taught me so much, Shia. I am so proud of you. I am so blessed to have you as my son. It is a true honor to be called your Momma. Thank you for being such a wonderful and amazing son. Until we meet again, know I love you deeply.

Momma

Running Again

I began running again, because all the tests came back, and my heart was functioning perfectly normal and showed no signs of stress despite the large amount of fluid around it. I was determined not to live in fear; rather, I would complete this difficult journey, fully relying and trusting in God. I had complete peace, but I also knew it would take courage once again to run.

I ran on a treadmill in our home. On the wall, hung a picture that my mom had bought for me years ago. The words, "Faith doesn't get you around adversity. It gets you through it," were a great encouragement as I focused on the picture while running. Just like in Hawaii, I was not alone in my journey. God was with me and always would be with me no matter the circumstances. I knew that He would get me through any adversity.

FAITH DOESN'T GET YOU AROUND ADVERSITY. IT GETS YOU THROUGH IT.

FAITH DOESN'T GET US AROUND ADVERSITY. IT GETS US THROUGH IT. "BE STRONG AND COURAGEOUS FOR THE LORD YOUR GOD WILL BE WITH YOU WHEREVER YOU GO." JOSHUA 1:9

BE STRONG AND COURAGEOUS FOR THE LORD YOUR GOD WILL BE WITH YOU WHEREVER YOU GO. JOSHUA 1:9

Chapter 14

SHIA'S EDUCATION & FUTURE

Spring 2017: The "Step Up" Program

Despite getting the revelation that my tight grip on Shia was causing intense waves of fear, I had a sense of freedom that God would truly care for Shia if I was no longer on this earth. Yet with Shia, God was still revealing areas I was struggling to fully trust Him. Maybe the possibility of not being in Shia's life, and God taking care of him, was easier to step into than trusting God to take care of Shia while I was present.

During that time, Shia was also getting in-home ABA therapy sessions. The supervisor had suggested that she thought Shia would do wonderfully in their program called Step Up. The only problem was that this program could only be offered in their clinic, and I was not allowed to go back in the room with him. Once again, I wanted control, so my peace left me when I thought of dropping him off for a couple of hours and not knowing what was going on.

This was much different from sitting in the waiting room for an hour when Shia was just a few feet away from me. Then I had the option to go in and attend the session at any point. But I could feel the tug on my heart. God wanted me to experience His freedom. He wanted to tend to this matter in my heart of not trusting Him fully with Shia's life. God was saying "Let go; trust Me. I have him. I have been guiding you. He is right where I want him. My plans are good."

The Step-Up program is designed to prepare children like Shia for public school. At this point, I planned to homeschool Shia, so why did he even need this program? I hesitated at first and reasoned that he didn't need this program, and that we should continue doing in-home sessions with me close by. Although this made me feel more comfortable, I knew deep in my heart that I was not surrendering. Once again, I was trying to control the situation. The supervisor told me about the many benefits this type of program could offer Shia, even if we chose not to send him to public school.

Staying in my comfort zone is not what had gotten me to the current level in my walk with God. My peace would leave every time I thought of Shia being away from me. After all, he could not communicate, and if someone was unkind to him in any way, how would I know? It was a tough place for me, and for Tim. We wanted to protect him in every way possible, but as I processed everything, I felt God remind me of what He spoke to me while in Hawaii, "Don't rootbound Shia." I knew immediately in my heart that I had to let the pot get bigger so Shia could grow and thrive even more.

I did let go, and at first it was painful. Shia attended sessions in the clinic for a couple of hours and seemed to be doing very well. It blessed me so much that he seemed to be thriving in this program. Then the supervisor suggested that we extend the sessions to four hours so he could get more of the Step-Up program. I was amazed that Shia still did very well. He was eager to go into the building, and he seemed happy when I picked him up. This made my momma's heart happy. After a short time, they suggested extending the time to a full eight hours to see how he would do. To my surprise, he was doing amazingly well, and God was doing an amazing work strengthening me during this time and steadying my walk in Him as I became peaceful being away from Shia.

Public School

Our walk of faith went deeper when I heard God speak, "I need you to send Shia to public school." I cried and fought intensely against it, which revealed yet another layer of fear and how much I still had a tight grip on Shia.

God was telling me to send Shia to public school, so why did I not trust that He had everything arranged for Shia's care as He thought was best? I was deeply uncomfortable. I found myself thinking of all the things that could go wrong. Once again, that weed of fear was choking out the truth found in God's word. God wanted me to experience freedom. He wanted the weeds gone, but was I willing to surrender to His will and trust Him?

One day, I was scrolling through social media and saw a posting that said, "Stop being afraid of what could go wrong and start being excited for what could go right." It hit me intensely that I was letting negative thoughts take over my mind, and that I wasn't even pondering the things that could go right. I had to go back and put my training into practice.

God's faithful encouragement was evident during the next seven days. Each day while scrolling through social media, He allowed me to see a version of the above quote every single day. Only God could have orchestrated that, and each time I heard Him say, "Shift your focus onto the good." It was powerful, and I was able to walk it out more steadily with peace in my heart.

A short time later, Tim shared his concerns about sending Shia to public school. He went through his long list of *what if this happens and what if that happens* and on and on. He was burdened by those thoughts just as I had been. I shared with him what God had done just the week prior and how it helped shift my focus and how it deeply encouraged me. That shift allowed me to find peace in knowing that I could trust God with all of it. It seemed to help Tim let go as well. Even though it was difficult stepping into this new chapter, we knew that God was with us every step of the way.

Summer 2017: A Praying Principal

I wanted to check out the school Shia would be attending. It was summer, but I had permission from the front desk to stop in. When I arrived at the school, I was praying as I walked to the front door, "God, if this is where Shia is supposed to go to school, then please show me while I am here."

Entering the school, I was immediately invited to sit and visit with the principal. She seemed preoccupied with her work when I first stepped into her office. I introduced myself and told her that I was checking out the school for my special needs son. As soon as I said, "special needs," I had her full attention. In fact, she lit up.

I shared my heart and nervousness about sending my child to public school. She was moved with great compassion and proceeded to share with me that special needs children have a special place in her heart. She then took me on a tour of the school and showed me the entire Exceptional Children's department. I was impressed with all the resources they had to offer Shia. As we walked, I told the principal that I was a praying momma and that I was praying if Shia was supposed to attend *this* school. She looked at me and said, "Just so you know…I am a praying principal. My eyes filled with tears as she spoke, and immediately I felt the Presence of God. Then I heard that still small voice saying, "I am here with this principal, and I will be here with Shia too. God continued to walk with me and revealed His Presence as He helped me to gradually let go of Shia and trust Him more deeply.

Fall 2017: Hand-Picked Shia's Teacher

Shia would be going into the Exceptional Children's Program, so I was required to attend a meeting to establish an Individualized Education Program (IEP) for Shia before he started school. During this meeting, I was very overwhelmed and very uncomfortable by all the information and the reality of what we were stepping into.

The "praying principal" and a few other teachers attended the meeting. The idea that I would soon be passing my child off to total strangers for a long period of time, five days a week, kept surfacing in my heart. I had to keep shifting my focus and whisper, "I trust you, God."

The meeting lasted a long time with a lot of information regarding Shia. At times I tuned it all out because I kept being drawn to the teacher who was leading the meeting. It was as though God was spotlighting her because I quickly noticed how knowledgeable she was and that she seemed to be very passionate. I sensed by her soft tone and gentle spirit that I should ask her some personal questions, so I asked how long she had been in the school. She had many years of experience, and all had been with special needs students. I felt in my heart that this teacher would be perfect for Shia.

Towards the end of the meeting, I felt a nudge in my heart to ask the "spotlighted" teacher some *more* questions. So, I mustered up the courage and asked, "Can you be Shia's teacher? She replied, while looking at the principal and said that she didn't know. By the end of the meeting, it had been decided that she would be Shia's teacher. I left that meeting overjoyed and felt that God had let me handpick Shia's teacher.

When I would drop Shia off at school and pick him up or attend school functions, I would see his teacher, Ms. Hatcher, interact with Shia. He absolutely loved her, and I could tell she cared greatly for him as well. It was a perfect fit, and once again, it was confirmation that Shia was exactly in the right place. Had God not guided us to purchase the home where we did, we might have not been blessed by this school with a praying principal and an amazing teacher.

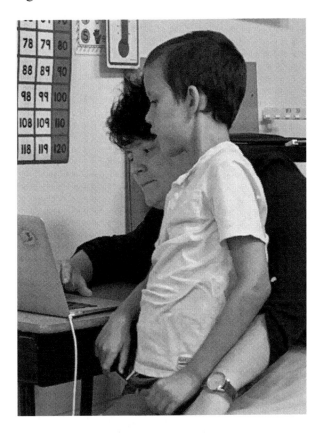

Thinking About Shia's Future

I needed to run to the grocery store while Tim and Shia stayed home. As I was standing in line, waiting to pay for items, I overheard the cashier, in pure frustration, telling the next person in line his frustration regarding a teenager. "It's not like it was hard. It was the easiest thing in the world." The customer nodded as if agreeing with the cashier, who was unprofessionally venting his frustrations.

The teen had to be around 13, but he was having a difficult time comprehending what the cashier was trying to say to him. As I was unloading my items, I could tell the cashier was getting frustrated that this kid was taking so long to grasp the simple instructions he was telling him. After a couple of minutes, the boy, without saying one single word, figured out what the cashier was saying and then proceeded to leave the store with his father who was standing at a distance.

After listening to the cashier vent his frustrations, I felt a need to say something to the cashier and to plant a seed. Being nervous and not wanting to embarrass him, I paid for my items and headed to the restroom. That still small voice kept saying, "Plant a seed." I did not want to cause a scene, because other people were around, but the still small voice nudged me again, "Plant a seed." I knew then I had to say something, no matter how I felt.

I left the restroom and walked straight towards the cashier and leaned in and said softly, "I heard what you said about that young man. It isn't easy for everyone, you know. I have a son who has a diagnosis, and he doesn't understand everything that is said to him." Embarrassed, the cashier stuttered over his words and said, "Um um, I wasn't talking about that." I just looked at him for a few moments. I couldn't say anymore as I was overtaken with emotion, so I walked away with tears filling my eyes.

Why did the grocery clerk incident affect me so much? I saw Shia in this teenager, and I saw the lack of compassion, grace, and patience the cashier had for him. I have dealt with many people like this cashier who were quick to make comments or give disapproving stares like they totally understood our situation.

Shia looks like any typical boy, but he isn't typical. Just like the young teen in the store wasn't typical, despite at first glance, you would have thought he was. Shia doesn't comprehend everything that is said to him and at this point, he is still almost completely non-verbal. You wouldn't necessarily think he was different from any other kid just by looking at him, but if you interact with him, you will discover he is a child that needs extra patience, grace, and compassion.

People are quick to make assumptions about my son's behavior, just like the cashier made in the grocery store. They assume that Shia is being disobedient, disrespectful, and uncooperative. Or they assume that he is dumb, not listening, purposely being difficult, or being a brat, who needs discipline.

Why didn't the father of this teenager say anything during this time or help his boy? Not that it is any of my business, but here are a few of my thoughts regarding that event.

I believe that the boy's father was allowing his son to make a purchase on his own to give him the opportunity to succeed on his own. He understands that he cannot protect his son from every rude comment, stare, or action from others. He believes that his son is capable of much more and needs to be given opportunities to succeed.

It is my job, as Shia's mother, to teach him the best way I know, how to be successful, strong, fearless, and courageous in this world where he will undoubtedly have opposition. I hope when Shia is 13, that I am confident enough in him to silently watch him struggle through something, that I could easily fix, but that he would want to do on his own, despite what the people around him are doing, thinking, and saying.

I have noticed that people become quickly offended or irritated when others are not doing things to their standards or moving at the pace they desire. I hope people can remember that there are those who have limitations and are struggling to do their best. For that reason, staring, judging, saying unkind words, being critical and offering "expert discipline" advice is hurtful and unnecessary. Rather, I would encourage people to build up each other. Treat others the same way they would want to be treated. Be kind and compassionate to one another. And always...Be Love and Give Love.

Chapter 15

THE NEW NORMAL

Late 2017: Preparing for the First Long Deployment

Tim was due to be away soon. This time it was different because he would be away much longer than in the past. One thing that God kept bringing to my heart was to face my fear of guns and get my concealed carry license. It was not so much for the purpose of carrying a weapon, but it was more for overcoming my fear. I wanted to be confident that if I needed to use a gun for protection, especially while Tim was gone, I would be capable of doing so.

A friend from church had offered concealed carry classes, so one day after church, I approached him. Fortunately, he was getting ready to teach another course, so I would be able to complete training prior to Tim leaving. I was surprised to discover that Tim was also thinking that I should take a concealed carry class. He was even surprised to see me talking to our friend about it without him having to encourage me to do so. I told Tim that God kept nudging me, so I felt it was time.

Tim was so proud of me that he took me gun shopping. He knew how afraid I was of guns and that this was a big step for me. Our friend was a great teacher and made me feel very comfortable and confident with my new gun. I passed his course and enjoyed shooting at different times with Tim and some of our friends from church. Thankfully, God provided all the support needed, and I felt a newfound freedom in overcoming another fear.

As the time got closer for Tim to deploy, I could feel God diving deeper into my heart, wanting to continue to free me of the things I still held with a tight grip. I believed that God led me to sit down and, in the stillness, encouraged me to let all-consuming thoughts fall away.

He spoke to my heart to be careful and not to fall into self-pity during this time of Tim's absence. I needed to press into God, so I could stand against fearful and negative thoughts that would only make this deployment harder.

God then warned me that as soon as I felt overwhelmed by day-to-day tasks, I should take a break, sit down with Him, and let Him refresh me. God reminded me that He daily walks with me and was calling me to do this in His strength and not my own. This was just another layer of deep trust that He wanted me to dive into with Him. I had a choice in how I would respond.

Getting Involved Again

Shia was in school and involved with therapy full time, so I had a lot of free time on my hands. I felt led to try to transfer my massage therapy license again. This time it was much easier than my failed attempts in Hawaii. I met all the qualifications, making it a very easy transfer. With the green light to move forward, I set up a room in our home as my massage therapy office and immediately started getting clients.

A church member asked me if I would do a study on my book, *Living Still,* which lasted several months. We walked through the book chapter by chapter. It was such a blessing to again be used by God to encourage, teach, and inspire others. It was because of the church that God led us to become involved in the community doing volunteer work and loving our neighbors in need.

God continued to bless with a couple more speaking opportunities, so I was excited to be back in my rhythm, which felt very similar to how things had been in Branson. It was wonderful to again be massaging, teaching, speaking, and giving back to the community.

A Great Teacher

One morning, my eyes were filled with tears as I drove away after dropping Shia off at school. His amazing teacher, Ms. Hatcher, had planned a long weekend trip with her mom, but to my great surprise, she was there and ready to greet Shia at the car and walk him to his room.

"Hey," I said to Ms. Hatcher. "I thought you weren't supposed to be here today." She answered, "I wasn't, but my two teacher assistants had emergencies that came up, so I postponed my trip with mom." She then proceeded to tell me, "The kids are too important. I couldn't leave them with three substitute teachers."

I do not expect teachers to put their lives on hold for our kids but being an Exceptional Children's teacher is different. The kids are used to routine and familiarity. His teacher knew this, and for her to make that sacrifice was beautiful and heartwarming.

Ms. Hatcher's sacrifice, her dedication, and her love for my precious Shia and all the other children in her class touched me deeply. With tears of gratitude, I drove away, thanking God for guiding us to this school and for blessing us with such a great and devoted teacher, who showed so much love to our little Shia.

Spring 2018: A Hard Deployment

I wrote in my journal, "This deployment has been hard. It seems that so many things are happening to try to derail me. My iPad stopped working and can't be fixed; my cell phone stopped working and can't be fixed; my laptop crashed and can't be restored; the garage door stopped working; something went wrong with the tire on my car; the kitchen sink started leaking; and Tim is gone, and all of this is on my shoulders to get fixed."

During these frustrating events, I was feeling weary, but my sweet Shia was in the other room singing. At this point, Shia still had little verbal communication with us, but he liked to sing. I peeked around the corner, and there I found him, sitting in his bed, singing at the top of his lungs, "I Surrender," a song that God had led him to find while his daddy was in basic training. Over and over, he sang his heart's desire to know God and to be completely surrendered to Him.

Tears streamed down my face as I listened to Shia singing. At that moment, I was reminded to surrender everything to God. I then made the decision to press forward, knowing that He would always be walking hand in hand with me.

A Home of Peace

Shia was in the public-school system's Exceptional Children's Program and was also attending a lot of therapy, so I was able to see many children like Shia. I was also able to see many parents interact with their special needs children. I have seen some beautiful things, but honestly, I have also seen more heartbreaking things.

One of the most heart-breaking scenes that I witnessed was while I was waiting in the car while Shia was in therapy. I overheard yelling just behind me at the entrance of one of the therapy buildings. Thankfully, it was not Shia's building. I couldn't help but turn around to see what was happening.

There was a car pulled up to the entrance. The door to the therapy building was propped open, and a lady was yelling very loudly, "Get in the car! Get in the f#@#ing car!" She kept yelling and cursing while pacing around her car. Sometimes she would hit the car in her anger and frustration. I had yet to see anyone else, so I wasn't sure who she was yelling at. With the therapy door still open, she got into her car and just sat there. It appeared that she was trying to calm down.

I immediately was moved with compassion because I understood her frustrations, and I felt in my heart to get out of my car and talk to her. But before I could even get out, she was already out of her car again and had walked in through the open door. Within a few minutes, I heard her saying repeatedly and loudly, "Get in the car!" I then saw her coming through the door pulling on a young man, probably 14 years old. He was struggling and resisting her while making stressful sounds and not forming words. She was continuing to yell at him while pulling on him. At one point, she finally dragged and shoved him into the back seat.

A lady from the building came out to assist her. It all seemed to be happening in slow motion, but it was very fast. Before I knew it, the mother had peeled out of the parking lot and sped down the road.

I went inside the therapy building where I found a couple of ladies, who worked there, in a complete daze. I told them I had just witnessed what had happened. They shared with me that it happened all the time. I shared my desire to help this momma in some way and then handed them my card to give to that momma in hopes she would contact me. She never did.

I got back in my car and sat there in tears, asking God why He allowed me to see what I had just witnessed. I heard His still small voice say that the greatest thing I could give a special needs child or any child for that matter...would be a home of peace.

Not all Children are Like Shia

I remember having a conversation with a lady who had been around Shia a lot as well as other special needs children. She always thought Shia was so chilled and peaceful. One day during a conversation she said to me, "You know Abby, not all children are like Shia." I said, "I know they aren't." But later that night I couldn't help but ponder some things deeply. I wondered how the tone of homes were for other special needs children who weren't as chilled as Shia. Was Shia so chilled and peaceful, because we have worked so hard to have and maintain a home of peace?

Thinking about those things made me more grateful that I had allowed and continue to allow God to tend to the deeper matters of my heart. It is only because of Him that I can walk in peace in the middle of autism. It is because of God that our home is peaceful and reflects His love and peace most of the time. However, we are not perfect, so there are times when that peace is disrupted, and we quickly see how that lack of peace negatively affects Shia.

Tim Returns Home

Tim returned from his long deployment, and we went on a vacation. It was nice to be back as a family again. As always, we just picked up where we left off and continued life together.

The vacation gave me a beautiful opportunity to reflect on where God had brought me in my journey. All the work He had done in my heart was truly making a difference. I was feeling much stronger and steadier and more stable in life.

Chapter 16

THINGS ARE CHANGING

November 2018: Things with My Heart Begin to Change

I continued to have routine echocardiograms, all of which were still showing my heart functioning normally, despite the large amount of fluid being present. Despite this, I started to experience heart palpitations. My heart would regularly skip a beat. At first, I didn't give it much thought, but as it continued for several weeks, I became more concerned but not fearful.

I went to my regular primary care doctor, who was aware of my situation and had looked over my medical records. She ran a few tests and scheduled a follow-up appointment soon after.

All the tests came back as normal. She reassured me that everything was fine. I was scheduled to get my routine echocardiogram soon, so we knew things would be checked from that angle as well. I left thinking all was okay.

I changed some things in my diet thinking they might have been the source of the palpitations, but those changes made little difference. Every day, many times a day, I was dealing with these skipped beats.

A nurse called saying that my echocardiogram appointment needed to be rescheduled for late January. I was a bit unsettled because I had not experienced these symptoms throughout my entire journey with the heart fluid. I was very concerned why the palpitations were still happening, so it was troubling to have the echocardiogram scheduled so far out. I knew that I needed to stand against the fear that was trying to rise within me. So, I pressed into God and felt His strength helping me to walk in faith, as I remembered all the ways He had been there for me since I had hit rock bottom in 2002.

Heading to Branson, Missouri, for Christmas

Despite having the daily palpitations, we felt led to head to Branson, to spend Christmas with my family. It is a 16-hour trip, but it was worth the drive. Being home for the holidays in Branson was so great. I cherish time with family, and Shia absolutely loves Branson. It was a wonderful time to decompress and be refreshed.

There is a unique feeling I experience every time I travel back to Branson. So many roots were established in Branson and so much personal growth happened there. I attended college. I met my husband and got married. Branson is where I hit rock bottom and where I blossomed out of that dark valley that I was living in. I wrote *Living Still* while living in Branson. I started my first business there and was heavily involved in the community. I got baptized with my husband at a church we loved. Shia was born in Branson. I had family and lots of friends there. Yet, I gave all of that up to follow the call God had for our family. It was beautiful to return and see even greater growth in my heart since leaving Branson in 2013.

138

Tim and I often wonder if we will return to Branson after his military career ends. Who knows, maybe one day I will open a Be Love Give Love store in Branson, Missouri. We shall see!!

January 2019: I See a Scene of Me Having Heart Surgery

The heart-palpitations were more frequent. As I was spending time with God and trying to quiet my mind and stay focused on Him, I saw a scene play out in my mind of me having heart surgery. This did not give me fear. Instead, I felt peace because I believed it was from God.

I told my husband and my holistic practitioner friend, with whom I had been sharing my journey, that I believed my situation had changed. Both said they were sure that I was fine, but I had a deep knowing that things were different.

I then heard God say, "Call and set up another appointment with your primary care doctor and demand to have an echocardiogram done." The original scheduling of the echocardiogram was not for three more weeks. Still peaceful, I called and was able to quickly get an appointment.

I shared with my doctor that I was still having palpitations, but they felt different and were more frequent. Despite my concerns, she tried to convince me that everything was good. After all, my blood pressure was normal, and my oxygen level was normal, and all my tests had come back normal. I then said I wanted an echocardiogram. She looked and noticed my last appointment had gotten rescheduled, and it had been many months since I had an echocardiogram done, so she decided to go ahead and order one. I was glad she did because I wasn't leaving that office until it was scheduled, because God told me to demand one. To my surprise, they scheduled me for the next day.

The echocardiogram was done at the military hospital since it was ordered by my primary care doctor and not the civilian cardiologist that was assigned to me off-post. I was prepared to get this echocardiogram, but I was also prepared to go straight to surgery. I knew something was different.

I also saw in my mind my fun, light-heartened friend from church being with me. I called her and shared a little bit of my situation and asked if she was available to go to my echocardiogram appointment with me. To my surprise, she wasn't available at the time of my appointment. I thought that was a bit odd, considering I thought God had shown me she would be with me at the hospital. I proceeded with the appointment, trusting that God was walking hand in hand with me, as He had so faithfully done in the past.

I felt steady and stable as I went into the appointment. While in the waiting room, I put my earbuds in and played a song that I had downloaded just a few weeks prior. It had deeply ministered to my heart and helped me stay focused on God, so I would not be swayed by this storm. This powerful song, "Peace Be Still," by The Belonging Co., and featuring Lauren Daigle, was a message to me, that regardless of the waves and storms, I was not to fear because God was right there with me. I felt Him strengthening me as I listened to the words and I could sense God giving me the command, through this song, to let my faith rise up within me. ("Peace Be Still" can be found on YouTube.)

They called me back. I felt a bit of fear, but then God powerfully spoke words He had spoken many times over the years. "Remember, courage is not the absence of fear. Courage is trusting Me and stepping forward with Me, despite what is trying to come against you. I am here, walking hand in hand with you. Do not be afraid. I have you covered under the shadows of My wings. You are strong and courageous in Me."

While getting the echocardiogram, I put my earbuds in and played on repeat the song, "Peace Be Still." Over and over, I let the words of that song minister to my heart, and I truly felt the Presence of God. I was not afraid. I was steady and stable. It was truly powerful. And then the echocardiogram was finished.

I dressed, and the technician walked me out to the waiting room and said goodbye. He was very professional and never gave any indication in his tone or body language that anything was wrong.

During the drive home, I was a bit perplexed that I wasn't rushed straight to the emergency room. I was thinking about the scene God had shown me of having heart surgery; however, trusting Him, I let those thoughts go.

January 17, 2019: The Call from The Cardiologist

With the feeling that something was still off, I was prepared to get a call from a cardiologist. In less than an hour from when I got home, my phone rang. I knew on the other end of the call would be a cardiologist. Before I answered, I said aloud to myself, "It's game time!"

I answered the phone, and the cardiologist introduced himself and asked immediately, but calmly, how I was feeling. I told him I was feeling fine. He then asked how my breathing was and a few other questions to which I was having no issues. I said, "I know I have a very large amount of fluid around my heart, and this is the first time you are seeing it." Again, he calmly answered, "Yes, you do, but things have changed. I need you to get to the emergency room very soon because you are in what is called tamponade."

At that time, I had no idea what tamponade meant, and the doctor didn't explain too much during our conversation. He just wanted me to quickly get to the emergency room. I felt perfectly fine, so I asked if I could pick up my special needs son from school and then drop him off at therapy. I briefly explained more of our situation with Shia, and he said, "I understand your concern, but I also need you to understand that your son needs his momma." The doctor then asked if I could get to the hospital within the next three hours. Although I said yes, I was not sure what was going to happen after those three hours. However, I had complete peace about taking care of my son first.

The cardiologist gave me his cell phone number and said to text him when I was on my way and when I arrived at the hospital. No matter the storms that come our way, we can never doubt God's goodness, faithfulness, and provision.

You would think by getting a call like this I would have panicked, but God had been refining my heart over the years and speaking so intensely to me, that He enabled me to be calm and in control of my emotions, despite being alone. My roots were deep in Him. I could feel His strength keeping me steady and stable in this storm. I was somewhat excited because God had already shown me what would be happening.

I finally reached my husband, then called my mom, and packed a bag for the hospital stay. I picked Shia up from school and dropped him off at therapy. I was overtaken with emotion and teared up when seeing Shia and then having to leave him at therapy. What-if thoughts washed over me, but quickly God comforted me and said, "I have Shia. I am with him as well."

I then met my husband at the house, and he drove me to the emergency room. Only God could have given me the ability to do this during this sort of news. As we drove the 30-minute drive to the hospital, Tim and I discussed all that was happening and how to move forward regarding who would take care of Shia until my mom arrived. She was on her way, but the trip was 12 hours.

Not just anyone can watch Shia. We knew we had a four-hour window where Shia was taken care of at therapy. My friend came to mind, who I thought was supposed to come with me to the echocardiogram appointment. I reached out to her and explained the situation and asked if she could be with me at the hospital a little later. That would allow Tim to take care of Shia. Without hesitation, she agreed. Though my timing was a little off, God had shown me that she would be with me.

I Was Stable

I walked into the emergency room and the cardiologist who had called me earlier met me at the entrance. He looked a little surprised, so I was not sure what he had expected. From that moment on, I felt I was being treated like royalty. The cardiologist walked me to the back, and they began to hook me up to monitors and draw blood and ask lots of questions and do a lot of other things that I can't even remember. I just remember many people around me and a lot of movement...a sort of chaos, but I was peaceful during all the activity.

They were surprised that I was stable, despite being in "tamponade." Since then, I found out that cardiac tamponade is a serious condition that occurs when extra fluid or blood builds up in the space between the heart and the pericardium, which is the sac around the heart. The extra fluid causes pressure on the heart, which keeps it from pumping enough blood to the rest of the body. A shorter definition is that the heart is beginning to collapse. Wow!!

My heart, blood pressure, oxygen level, and all tests came back normal. This was something the cardiologist had never seen. No

144

wonder he was so surprised when he saw me walk into the emergency room. I guess with the severity of my situation, he believed I would be gasping for air and certainly not walking and talking.

Since I was stable, they decided to do surgery the next morning, so they could have the entire cardiac team available, instead of doing surgery late that night. I just loved hearing those words that I was stable. I did, in fact, feel stable on so many levels. What an amazing manifestation of God to have me be miraculously stable physically, emotionally, and spiritually in what many would call a dire situation. God knew that the deep desire of my heart was to be stable and steady in each storm, then people could be drawn to Him when seeing His strength working in me.

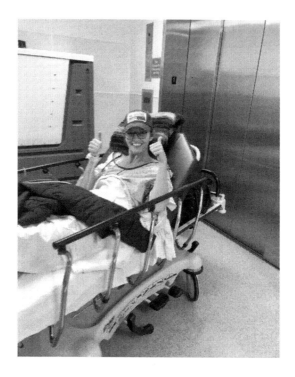

God Provides

Let me tell you how God was in the details of all of this to provide all our needs. Tim was home and not deployed. He also had a four-day weekend, so he didn't have the stress of being behind on work. The decision to move surgery to the next morning, gave my mom just enough time to get from Missouri to be with Shia, so Tim could be with me. My fun, light-hearted friend hung out with me till about 10 p.m. the night before surgery. We had so much fun laughing, getting the staff to dance, and just being silly. We decided the staff should refer to me as Princess. God knew I needed Christy to keep the atmosphere full of joy that night before surgery. Laughter is truly the best medicine.

After Christy left, I was alone, but I was peaceful. My dad called and said some very special words to me, "God is not finished with you yet. Everything is going to be okay." It was comforting for my Dad to confirm what I already knew deep in my heart. The visions spoken in 2007 had not yet come to pass, and I believed and did not doubt that those visions would become a reality.

I also texted family and friends who were reaching out to me, and I talked with my mom for a little bit while she was driving to be with us. Although sleep eluded me, I was steady in my faith, stable in my walk, securely fixed in God, and peaceful in my heart.

I had never been in an emergency room. I had previously had the pericardial tap procedure and had my wisdom teeth removed, but I had never had a major surgery. Now I had wires attached all over me along with several IVs.

147

Lying on the hospital bed, I felt God draw me back in remembrance of His faithfulness throughout my entire journey. I listened to those songs that He had brought me during the last several years that were used to encourage and comfort me. I let the word of these songs penetrate my heart deeply. I felt God's Presence powerfully. I knew He had me under the shadow of His wing, and my hand was in His. Instead of letting the storm have me, I just let go and felt myself being held by the loving hands of God. Although I had moments of feeling the intensity of the situation, I was not swayed because He overwhelmed me with His strength, courage, and peace.

I came through the surgery beautifully with no complications, but I was still having the same palpitations. The cardiologist told me to give it some time, because my heart had gone through a lot.

A pericardial window surgery is a procedure where a small hole is made in the sac of the heart so if any fluid continues to build up, it can drain. They also put two tubes in the pericardial sack around my heart to allow fluid to drain, which took a total of five days. I was then left with about a three-inch cut in the center of my chest and two smaller ones where the tubes had been. Each day, my scars are a beautiful reminder of God's faithfulness.

I stayed in the hospital for a week. During that time, I connected to many staff members working with me, shared my love for God, encouraged hearts that needed to be encouraged, made new friends, and was able to be a light during the storm. Also, while in the hospital, they continued to run many tests to try to determine, once again, why there was fluid around my heart in the first place. I immediately chose to put those results into God's hands, despite the palpitations. I was walking my journey with His peace and trusting His plan for my life. Although I did not know what the future held, I did know, with absolute certainty, that God held my future in His hands.

Leaving The Hospital

I had never spent a night away from Shia until I was admitted into the hospital. I spent seven nights away from him...never getting to see him. Tim and I felt it would be best for him not to come to the hospital to see me. We knew Shia would have obsessively tried to take off everything that was attached to me because it was different, like the IVs, wires, tubes, etc. Different isn't always better when it comes to autism.

When I got home, I had the sweetest moment with Shia. I walked into his bedroom where he was sitting on his bed playing and knelt beside his bed. Shia just looked at me. He then reached out and touched my face while he continued to stare at me. Tears filled my eyes. Despite his inability to verbally communicate, his touch beautifully expressed his thoughts and feelings of love.

Follow Up Appointments

All the tests they ran came back negative once again, and they began to label all of this as being idiopathic, which means an unknown cause, but they wanted to keep doing some tests and continue monitoring my heart with regular echocardiograms. I was hopeful, despite the continuing daily palpitations, which all tests showed to be harmless.

I remember at one of my follow-up appointments talking to the cardiologist that oversaw my surgery. He had become my official cardiologist, so I asked him how I was able to endure my heart collapsing without having true symptoms of it occurring. He answered, "Because you are a strong, healthy woman, your body was able to compensate." At that moment I was reminded of this verse, "My flesh and heart may fail, but God is the strength of my heart and my portion forever" (Psalm 73:26 NIV).

I am so grateful that I had a beautiful foundation built by God. That foundation taught me how to care for myself, which I shared in *Living Still*. Otherwise, my story might have had a different ending. I might have died of sudden cardiac arrest just as it was spoken over me. Instead, to this day, I can stand in awe of God's faithfulness.

It is All Worth It

I am thankful that my heart issues challenged me to trust God more deeply during those very stormy and difficult days. I can say that my journey was worth the suffering, for it was in that suffering that my roots in God grew so much deeper as He was working it all together for my good. I would do this all over again just to experience the depth of faith and trust I now have in God. I am even more confident now that He will never desert me, never give me up, never leave me without support, never leave me helpless, never forsake me, and He will never let me down or relax His hold on me (Hebrews 13:5-6).

150

Pockets of Fluid Still around My Heart

One month after surgery the results from my first echocardiogram sent me into yet another spiritual workout. I was hopeful all was clear, but now I had to do another cardiac MRI, stress test, and seven-day heart monitor. They wanted to get more data because the echocardiogram showed pockets of fluid around my heart, and I was still having palpitations.

The doctor said that more than likely the problem was due to the chronic effusion (fluid around my heart) that I had for so many years. And that can sometimes cause the sac around the heart to stick to the actual heart, creating a pocket. After the MRI, stress test, and monitor, my cardiologist wanted to see me again and then go from there. I was a bit discouraged and weary, as I had been so hopeful that this would be over. Yet there I was having to do another spiritual workout.

While driving home from my appointment, I was listening to the radio when God again revealed Himself through a powerful song that penetrated my heart and gave me the jolt I needed to keep persevering and trusting in Him. I purchased the song, "Even Then" by Micah Tyler and listened to it often.

Each time, the song gave me the boost I needed to keep going, while focusing completely on God and trusting Him no matter how things would end. After all, I had no place to go but to Him and no place to run except into His arms. At times it felt as though this was never going to end. I knew God would never let me go. I knew that even in the middle of this battle that He alone was my defense. No matter how it ended, He was with me. (Go to YouTube to see the beautiful lyrics and hear the music.)

I was pleased to find out that all the tests my cardiologist had ordered came back perfectly normal.

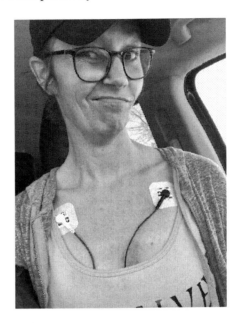

May 2019: Burden on My Heart

The journey continued with having palpitations four months after surgery. So, they decided to have me wear another heart monitor. This heart monitor testing showed the palpitations were placing a slightly increased but low burden on my heart. I was then put on a different medication because the one I was on was not working to help decrease the palpitations. They also suggested that I consider getting an implantable heart monitor that would record my heart 24/7.

The doctors decided to send me to an endocrinologist and a gastroenterologist to rule things out and send me back to the rheumatologist as well. They were trying to determine the cause of the fluid and why I continued to have palpitations every day.

The results from my latest routine heart echocardiogram came back normal, so that was good news. All I could do at that point was continue trusting God and keep persevering. He had brought me this far, and I knew He would continue to walk with me.

Tim Left for Another Longer Deployment

In the middle of all that was still happening with my heart, Tim had to leave for another long deployment, yet I was peaceful with him leaving. With each separation from Tim, God had worked intensely in my heart, and I sensed a deeper strength, confidence, and steadiness.

Something beautiful would happen when Tim was away; Shia would flow with it. Fear, worry, or sadness would never overtake him. Maybe it is because this is what he has known since he was two, but then again, Shia had always been like that from the very start when Daddy left for basic training.

It was evident that God was protecting Tim and Shia's bond, because they always picked up right where they left off. Tim and I have always been so grateful for that and for the steadiness in Shia that God gifted him.

Chapter 17

GOD'S SOLUTIONS

Picky Eater

Shia is an extremely picky eater. It comes with sensory processing disorder. We had tried food therapy, which wasn't successful. I was starting to get really concerned about nutritional deficiencies in Shia but felt in my heart to pray about it, release it, and trust that God would help me in this situation, as He has so faithfully done in the past.

I was hoping that God would give Shia the courage to try new foods but that never happened. However, what did happen was that over the course of about two weeks, I heard about this whole food product, not once, not twice, but three times, so I thought this would be perfect for Shia and an answer to prayer.

I was overjoyed with this one simple solution God had brought to us. Previously, God had led me to use syringes with Shia's supplements when we lived in Hawaii, so I did this with the new food product. It was effortless. I simply broke open the capsules that were filled with high-quality whole food in a powder form, mixed them with water, drew the mixture into a couple of syringes, squirted it into his mouth, and chased it with water. Shia took them like a pro, which gave me peace of mind about Shia's nutrition.

We still try new foods, but this momma's heart is confident that he is getting nutrition from a wide variety of fruits and veggies every day.

A short time later, I felt led to try the whole food shake mix from the same company, and Shia loved it. Each morning he drank it on the way to school, which reassured my heart even more that Shia was getting his nutritional needs met. God continued to guide me and walk with me in all areas of my life.

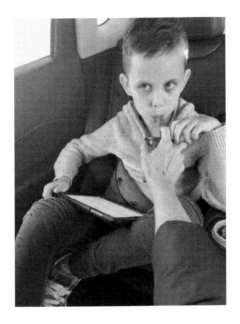

Others Engaging with Shia

One day at church, Shia and I were sitting outside on a bench when a friend walked up and said to Shia, "Hi." And then he quickly walked away. A short time later, he came back and said, "I am sorry, Abby. I just don't know how to engage with Shia." I replied, "That is okay. I completely understand."

I remembered when we lived in Missouri that I had a massage client who was completely nonverbal. Honestly, I was uncomfortable each session because I didn't know how to engage with him. I think about those sessions a lot and have empathy for others that find it awkward to engage with Shia. But then I think about all the required therapy that helps Shia navigate and engage in our world. That causes me to wonder about that missing link that could teach a typical person how to engage in the world with all special needs individuals.

It is rare to see a typical person, unless professionally trained or has experience with special needs individuals try to engage with Shia. Most of the time, people stare at him as if he is a zoo animal on display to be stared at and make comments. Thankfully, God has done a deep work within my heart, so this doesn't bother me nearly as much as it once did. I see past the stares and comments, and I realize there is a missing piece, because they have never been taught how to be love and to give love to special needs individuals. I hope that changes in the future.

Summer 2019: Shia is Growing and Things are Changing

Later that same year, as Shia was getting older, it seemed the diagnosis of sensory processing disorder was affecting him more. All his senses became more heightened, especially to any kind of negative and intense energy from screens, which terrified him.

Screens are everywhere...gas pumps, big-screen billboards, waiting rooms, churches, stores, restaurants, computers, and I have seen screens in public bathrooms. Everyone is carrying smartphones and tablets. This made going out in public extremely difficult for us. Additionally, Shia's expressive/receptive language disorder makes it difficult for me because he doesn't understand everything that is said to him. Nor is he able to verbally express why he feels the way he does. But as I relied on my training, trusted in God, and continued to run the race He set before me, I felt Him comforting and encouraging us.

I remember an appointment where I first noticed Shia's sensitivity to these different stimuli. We walked into the waiting room, which had multiple televisions. Many people were on their phones and tablets. Shia wanted to leave immediately, but we couldn't. This appointment was necessary for a therapy referral for him. So, I scanned the area to find a place where Shia could feel safe, and I could try to calm him down.

I found a space under the water fountain where he could hide and not see all the screens. I sat with him on the floor while he calmed down, then I checked him in, which was just a few feet away. People were staring, but thankfully God had worked on my heart regarding what people thought, and at that moment, I didn't care. Shia w as my only concern in helping him cope in a very noisy and stimulating place. I thought, *No wonder this kid loves to be outside any chance he can, so he can get away from it all.*

He seemed content under the water fountain while we waited for them to call our name. But when we were led back to the doctor's examining room, Shia immediately spotted the screen on the blood pressure machine and instantly became fearful and wanted to leave.

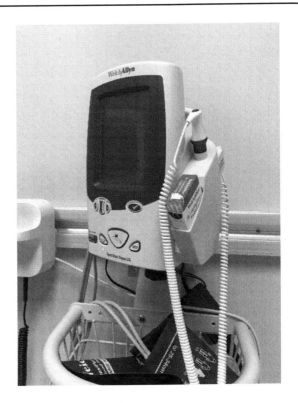

There was no way to avoid the blood pressure machine because it was in plain sight. I then felt God guiding me to reach inside my purse to find something to redirect his focus. Although it wasn't raining that day, for some reason, I had an umbrella in my purse. When I pulled it from my purse, he immediately focused on it. I told Shia we could open it so he could hide under it. I then turned on some piano music that was on my iPhone. (He is fine with screens he can control.) As he listened to the music, he became a changed little boy. Out of sight, out of mind.

Shia became very happy and content. He felt safe and was able to calm down under the umbrella, which reminded me of the big umbrella tree in Hawaii where God had spoken to me and said, "I will hide you under the shadows of My wings."

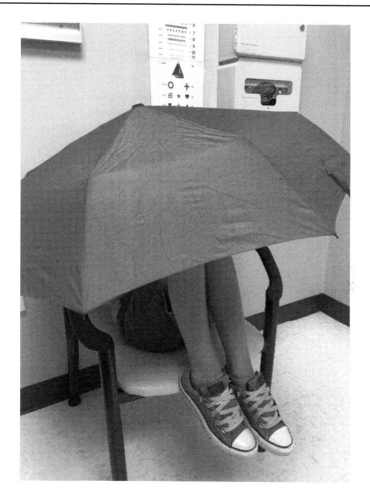

We live in a world of technology, so it is impossible to avoid screens. You see them everywhere you turn, which makes getting out in public very challenging for the Lewis family. There is a park that we go to where a large lighted billboard can be seen. This lighted sign changes ads every few seconds. So, when we go to this park we have to play where trees are covering the sign. If Shia happens to see the screen, he becomes fearful, so we calmly redirect him and continue to enjoy the park.

Screens were everywhere in the church we attended, making it extremely uncomfortable for Shia. It finally reached the point where he didn't want to walk through the doors of the church. It was so painful watching him struggle, that for his sake, we decided it was best to stop attending church.

Chapter 18

TRUSTING GOD
IN ALL SITUATIONS

Fall 2019: Back to My Heart

All the tests ordered by numerous doctors came back negative. I was still having palpitations almost every day. The new medication slowed down the palpitations, but it did not stop them completely. The medicine also made me very sleepy, which I didn't like. After some time in prayer, I didn't believe that having the implantable monitor was the route I should take.

The medical staff had exhausted any and every explanation for my heart palpitations. Their testing had not revealed the reason for these annoying things that were not harming me. It was like having someone tap on your shoulder every day to let you know they were still there.

My cardiologist told me he had done all that he knew could be done. He had given me a clean bill of health and told me to come back in a year to get another echocardiogram. And if all was clear, then I would be fully released from cardiac care. He then said, "Go, enjoy and live your life."

Still knowing my body was giving me signs that something was not right, I felt led to reach out to my holistic practitioner friend, Ashley, located in Missouri and ask her questions. She referred me to a lady who was closer, about two hours, and who did the same kind of testing as Ashley. However, this was a different type of testing that none of the medical doctors had run, and it wasn't covered by our insurance. Nonetheless, we felt it was the next step to take and moved forward, hoping to finally have answers.

The results of her testing showed an imbalance in my minerals despite my blood work showing they were all in the normal range. So, she put me on a high-quality mineral complex and a few other things to help bring balance back to my body. I talked to my cardiologist, and he agreed to try this and told me I could stop taking the medication he had prescribed. I was excited that I would no longer be sleepy all the time.

I didn't see a big shift immediately but over time, I noticed a difference in the palpitations. I was told to give my body time to rebalance itself because my body had been through a lot and would take some time to heal. I was grateful that I had listened to the prompting of the Spirit and had not moved forward with the implantable heart monitor.

Letting go of Tim

Tim was going through another intense season. And being a natural encourager and teacher, I wanted to help him. However, Tim wasn't asking for my help. Despite that, I was constantly giving him all sorts of advice and trying to fix the problem. My heart hurt for him, and I deeply wanted to help him find peace in the middle of his trial. Unfortunately, what I was doing was only causing both of us a great deal of frustration.

I remember as I was sharing some of my heart with my dear friend Deneé, she felt led to share a story that she believed would encourage me. As she was talking, I clearly heard that still small voice saying, "Do you want to do this, or do you want Me to?" I knew God was asking me to let Tim fully go and to trust that He would faithfully encourage, guide, and strengthen him just as He had and continues to do with me.

It wasn't easy to let go of Tim. I had to rely on my training to lay this burden down. I remember many times just stepping away and crying while praying and asking God, "Help me trust You with Tim and to let him go. My heart wants to help him find peace, but I know You are far more capable of helping him than I am. Help me have the strength to persevere in this as You work in him. Help me to be quiet and only speak words of encouragement and wisdom as You prompt me to speak. Help me be the helpmate that You need me to be for Tim and to focus on all the good in him."

Letting Tim go was another spiritual workout as I made every effort to speak only when God prompted me to speak. I could feel God deepening my roots in Him as I trusted Him with the deeper matters of Tim's heart.

November 2019: Shia Feels Energy of Others

Thank goodness for spinning stools in doctors' offices where Shia doesn't like to go. Things like this make it more enjoyable for him and distract his overstimulated mind from the not-so-fun things when he is out in public, especially at doctors' offices.

Shia had a routine eye appointment that required getting dilating drops in his eyes. He struggled with screens, but by the grace of God, we were able to hide from them, so Shia was calm while waiting. But during this appointment, I saw Shia do something I had never seen before.

Over the years, as I have watched Shia, I have noticed that he senses and responds to things within people, who are not peaceful. And I have noticed how he has acted when the tone of our home or other places we visited were not peaceful. I thought maybe it was a gift God had given him, or maybe it was because of the sensory processing disorder. Either way, at this appointment, he had an intense reaction.

Shia was happily spinning on the chair in the examining room when the doctor and her assistant entered and said hello. Everything about Shia immediately changed, and with great intensity, he did something I had never seen him do. He got up from playing on his spinning chair and ran to the door, desperate to leave. He was greatly distressed, so I tried to calm him down, but my efforts were not working.

The doctor and assistant tried to get closer to him, which only made things worse, so I suggested they give me a minute. They silently stared from a slight distance as Shia was frantically pulling on the doorknob. He just wanted to get out of there. I had never seen this type of behavior in him.

I remained completely calm and peaceful, reassuring Shia he was okay and that I was with him. Then I heard that still small voice say, "Shia, feels what is going on inside of people." I immediately looked at both women and said, "Shia is picking up on something from one of you." Neither said a word but stared as I went back to trying to calm Shia down.

Maybe what I said shifted something, because Shia calmed down slightly, but I could tell he was still extremely uncomfortable and standing close to the door. The doctor then said, "This will only take a minute." She proceeded to get close to Shia, quickly looked into his eyes, and within a couple of minutes she left the room.

What happened next was confirmed in my heart about Shia's ability to sense things within people. The assistant was still in the room, but now that the doctor was no longer in the room, Shia immediately calmed down and was back to spinning on the chair. I told the assistant that Shia had picked up on something that was going on within the doctor. The assistant said she understood completely and shared that she had seen that similar behavior in a special needs family member.

The Gift of Sensitivity

I don't have a diagnosis of autism or sensory processing disorder, but I have the gift of sensitivity. This is an area where I can deeply empathize with Shia. I have a heightened sensitivity to certain sounds and smells and like Shia, I am sensitive to the environment around me. I pick up on the same positive and negative energy flowing through people and intensely feel the darkness within the world and within others.

Unlike Shia, I have learned how to process all that I am feeling, and I know how to stand steady and stable in the situation. Shia's only defense is to escape from it all. I can't imagine how he must feel in public places where there are a lot of people. Maybe that is why God has given me such a deep passion for spreading the message of Be Love Give Love. We need to meet people where they are and inspire them to let God work on the deeper matters of their heart. Then more of God's light and love can flow through them and greatly impact the world around them.... the world my precious Shia lives in.... the world we all live in.

Chapter 19

STRUGGLE
AND ADJUSTMENT

Break-Ins

During Tim's long deployment of 2019, there were a lot of break-ins in our subdivision. I found this out on our neighborhood Facebook community page. For what seemed to be weeks, I would read stories about people's cars getting broken into at night and some houses as well.

You would have thought that my reaction to these break-ins would have scared me and caused sleepless nights. But because of the deep work God had done in my heart over the years, I was standing firm. I was steady, peaceful, and stable. I trusted God and I was confident in my ability to use a gun if I had to. I slept peacefully with a loaded gun close by… just in case.

I was amazed at how far God had brought me, and I found myself often pondering my journey and the deep healing that had happened in my heart. It is amazing what God can do when we fully surrender to Him and allow Him to tend to the matters of our hearts.

Tim Returned Home

Tim returned home and we traveled to Oklahoma City to visit friends and family for the holidays. Shia struggled a lot more on this trip with all his heightened senses and the fear of screens. He struggled to go into the homes of our friends and family with all the stimulation of people's energy, noise, and screens. He was more comfortable sitting by the door with his iPad, a screen he could control, and wait patiently until it was time to go.

Tim and I communicated about the situation and agreed that Tim would stay and visit, and Shia and I would head back to the hotel where he would feel calmer. I was completely fine with that because it was Tim's side of the family and friends he had grown up with.

My main concern was for Shia to be calm and peaceful. God carried us through and gave us some good moments outside for Shia to completely escape from it all.

Tim Opens Up About His Struggles

I continued to be diligent in letting go of Tim and trusting God to tend to the deeper matters of his heart. And as I did, I began to see a tremendous breakthrough in him. He was walking in more peace as he learned to let go and trust God with the burdens that he had been carrying for so long.

Tim is an internal processor, a very quiet man, and a profound thinker. The deeper the issue, it seems the longer he needs to sit with his thoughts. To be honest, I was getting impatient and wanted him to share, so I could help him find peace in whatever was causing him to carry such a heavy weight. But in those frustrating moments, I always heard the still small voice reminding me what He had spoken to me earlier in our journey. "Do you want to do this, or do you want Me to?" As I let go of Tim and trusted God to tend to his heart, something began to change within him, and eventually he revealed what he had been struggling with so intensely.

Tim was deeply concerned about Shia's future and wondered if he would be able to have a wife and kids, and if not, who would take care of him after we were no longer here to provide and care for him. That was and is a heavy burden to bear, so I understood why he was so weighed down by it for so long.

I also had similar thoughts when I was told I could die of sudden cardiac arrest. So, I shared with Tim the same things that God had spoken to my heart. I knew God deeply cared about Shia and that He would provide for him if we were no longer on this earth to care for him. God's plans are good for Shia, just as they are good for us. With this new understanding of Tim's concerns, we were both able to walk in more peace as we chose to trust God to lead and guide us in knowing how to navigate Shia's future.

Mom Had a Wreck

January of 2020, my mom was in a car accident. Thankfully she was okay, but she had to have surgery on her ankle and would not be able to put weight on it for several weeks. She needed a lot of assistance, so I dropped everything, and Shia and I immediately went home to Missouri to care for her. We stayed for two weeks,

174

then my siblings and other family members helped to care for her. Shia and I returned a couple of weeks later and stayed for another two weeks. Shia did very well during this visit, because for the most part, it was just mom, Shia, and me.

I was completely disconnected from my normal life back in North Carolina. As a result, I had so much time to pray and ponder things on the 12-hour drives to and from Missouri. I started to feel a disconnect from massage therapy, and I also felt a deeper stirring in my heart to get the Be Love Give Love message into the world. I had been stepping out with it a little in the fall of 2019, but I had no idea how to move forward with it.

Chapter 20

GOD OPENS DOORS AND HEARTS

Birthing of be Love Give Love Product Line

The desire to have a Be Love Give Love product line was birthed in my heart when my mother-in-law made me a shirt with my Be Love Give Love logo on it and sent it to me as a gift while we lived in Hawaii. Seeing the logo on a shirt did something in my heart, and from that day, I found myself praying and wondering if I would have a Be Love Give Love product line and maybe a Be Love Give Love store someday.

My mom knows that I love to wear hats. So, as a thank you for helping her during her recovery from the accident, she wanted to bless me with a couple of hats with my logo on them.

She knew a local lady in Sikeston, Missouri, who owned a boutique that offered an assortment of items. So, one day after one of mom's follow-up doctor's appointments, she said that we should go to the shop. When we pulled in front, mom suggested that I go into the shop, and she and Shia would wait in the car.

Meeting and chatting with the owner of the store and sharing what Be Love Give Love is all about was a great joy. When I heard her reaction, everything shifted within me. It gave me a deeper desire to move forward with the Be Love Give Love product line and begin the process of stepping away from massage therapy.

March 2020: Covid Changes Everything

Everything was upside down in the world when I arrived home from my last trip to Missouri. COVID had happened. Thankfully, after years of experiencing the ever-changing military life, it became relatively easy to flow with the sudden changes that COVID brought. The pandemic forced me to quit massaging, which was beautiful because God had already given me a disconnect from that career. Shia was now home and attempting to do virtual school with me, but I quickly realized that virtual school would not work for him, because of his fear of screens.

Shia was in the Exceptional Children's Program, so he was able to keep the same teacher for the first five years of school until he transferred to another building. So, with the help of his amazing teacher, Ms. Hatcher, we were able to present school to Shia in a different way.

Ms. Hatcher basically taught me how to teach Shia. I would follow her instructions and then report his progress to her. I was becoming Shia's teacher, and he and I were doing very well as I applied what I had learned from all of Shia's therapists and Ms. Hatcher. I was very confident in what I was called to do during that season. Little did I know the reason for God building my confidence to teach Shia.

Be Love Give Love Product Line Launched

My massage room was converted into my Be Love Give Love office. When it was possible, I worked on getting the Be Love Give Love product line launched. The connection I had made with the lady in Missouri was amazing. She gave me all her contacts and suppliers she had used for so many years and told me exactly what to do. I was amazed that God just handed everything to me. I just needed to trust Him, take the step of faith, and invest in it.

Tim and I talked and prayed about the investment, and he gave me his approval to move forward. So, I courageously stepped out in faith and launched the Be Love Give Love product line and online store. I also launched the Be Love Give Love podcast in July of 2020.

The deep desire that had been in my heart for so many years was unfolding right before my eyes. As I continued to live a surrendered life, God was faithfully leading, guiding, and walking this journey hand in hand with me.

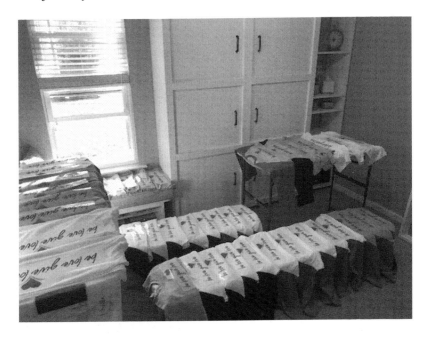

Keeping My Priorities in Line

I love to work. I love to create. I love to teach and inspire others, and during that season I was getting to do all of that with the release of the Be Love Give Love product line and podcast. I was enjoying it so much that I had to rely on my training to focus on God, maintain my priorities, and adjust to the flow of this new season in my life.

I work completely from home. Many times, it was insanely tempting when I was in an energy flow of creating and working, to push things aside that needed to be done for the home and for

Tim and Shia. However, I knew that God didn't want me to neglect home and family for the purpose of working on what He had blessed me with. If God was going to continue to bless this venture, and if there was going to be peace and order in our home, I had to be very mindful to keep my priorities in order. The bottom line was and is that my family and home will always be my priority.

Be Love Give Love Markets

After talking with Tim, I strongly felt led by God to venture out on some Saturdays, while he was off work and home spending daddy-son time with Shia. This would allow me to move forward with God and set up the Be Love Give Love booth, where my volunteers and I could have the opportunity to spread love to everyone that crossed our path. My hope is that people will experience the power of the Be Love Give Love message. That life-changing message is simply loving people just as they are and allowing God to do the work in their hearts.

My prayer has been that this message of love ignites a spark within hearts, and God turns that spark into a flame that burns brightly and impacts countless lives. As I thought about the many lives that could be touched by Be Love Give Love, I couldn't help but reflect on the Wildfire Vision of 2007 that said there would be pockets of fire, growing like wildfire across the world.

My greatest desire is to shine God's light so brightly that people feel the warmth of His love reaching out and embracing them. That is why my volunteers and I focus on spreading love to anyone and everyone who comes to our booth. If they buy some of our merchandise to help spread the message of love, then that is great. But more importantly, we want people to feel the love and light of God.

People who visited our booth would ask, "What is Be Love Give Love?" We would respond, "Be Love Give Love is a way of life. We are all about spreading God's love and lighting up the world as we meet people right where they are and love them unconditionally." So often their response would be, "The world could really use a lot more of that."

Why Be Love Give Love Began

People would often ask how the concept of Be Love Give Love began. We would give them the following Be Love Give Love story.

I know someone who at their lowest point in their life, when all seemed hopeless and dark, was judged, criticized, shamed, preached at, had Jesus thrown in their face, pushed aside, feared, and ignored. I also know someone in the exact same situation who was seen, loved unconditionally, accepted just as they were, embraced, heard, encouraged, and had seeds gently placed into their heart by some beautiful people, like Matt Ranker, Founder of We Shall See. So, which one do you think continued down a dark, painful road? Which one do you think felt the unconditional love of God? Which one do you think went on to fully transform their life?

183

The two people are the same person...ME, Abby Lewis, founder of Be Love Give Love. I believe with everything in me that the way we treat others deeply matters. The moment we choose who to love and who not to love, we have completely missed the heart of God.

I was asked one day, what kind of organization Be Love Give Love was and I replied, "It isn't really an organization; it is a way of life."

I was deeply moved by the impact Be Love Give Love was having on people at the markets. I noticed over and over that our booth became a safe place for some people to share and cry, as we embraced them, just as they were. It touched my heart deeply that people felt welcomed, loved, accepted, and safe when they were around our Be Love Give Love booth.

When you truly meet people right where they are, and receive them with open arms and unconditional love, a.k.a. Be Love Give Love, it draws people near and makes them feel safe. They trust you and open their hearts to you. That is when healing takes place within their soul. Light overtakes the darkness. Love conquers all.

Having experiences as I did at the markets, I couldn't help but ponder what God might have in store for the future of Be Love Give Love. I believe that the world needs more love, which requires that we be love so we can give love. I continue to dream big and pray hard that God will use Be Love Give Love in a mighty way to greatly impact the world we live in.

Chapter 21

ADJUSTMENTS AND BLESSINGS

Covid Continues

The negative energy of the world heightened as COVID continued, and my poor Shia was struggling intensely in public places and picking up on all of it. He would cry hysterically in parking lots making it impossible for me to enter any public places with him. I cannot imagine what he feels in a place where there are so many people who have been impacted by COVID. The

stress of the pandemic created so much fear, worry, bitterness, sadness, anger, and so much more that Shia was able to pick up on all those emotions.

So, we had to again adjust to life and the circumstances of COVID. All of Shia's ABA sessions became in-home sessions. I stopped taking him anywhere in public where there were a lot of people. It was just too much for him to process, although we would do quick trips into places that only had a small amount of people. We had hoped that fewer people would help him adjust better, but he still struggled greatly.

Thankfully with all my training in being still with God, and all the work He did in the soil of my heart, I was able to continue to let go, adjust, and flow peacefully with what God had us doing. Shia was now home with us 24/7. But God faithfully provided friends to run errands for me if Tim was gone. I did almost all the grocery shopping online, and would pick up groceries using their curbside service.

The pandemic did not prevent us from moving forward. I was able to work while Shia did his in-home therapy. Because God is our amazing Provider, He provided a friend who had many years of experience with special needs children. If Tim was not available, she would come to our home and watch Shia so I could step away and take care of other things. God, in His faithfulness, always took care of our every need, and we adjusted beautifully.

Be Love Give Love Grows

I quickly outgrew my small Be Love Give Love office, but I was content, happy and making do with the space God provided. When we are grateful for what we do have, I believe that God honors our heart's desire. So, one day while Shia and I were away from the house, Tim surprised me by rearranging the house to give me the biggest room in the home for my new Be Love Give Love office. I was blown away and so excited that God had spoken my need to Tim, and he willingly blessed me with a new and larger space.

God Blows Me Away

God blew me away again!! Be Love Give Love was deeply blessed by my good friend Lisa, who is a truck driver and travels all over the United States. At no expense to me, she asked if she could put our trademarked logos on her truck. I was blown away and absolutely thrilled and said, "Of course!" I quickly worked on designing the perfect color to match her beautiful purple truck and her free-loving personality.

Lisa posted pictures of her truck on social media and said, "This truck is dedicated to Be Love Give Love, for Abby. I hope to spread her message across our beautiful country, and I hope that it can change the hearts of people…even if it is just one person each day. Daily spreading the message of love and being kind to another human being is what this is all about. Just one gesture a day.

I have great peace in my life. I love to smile at people and give them a little kindness and do something nice for someone. God, peace, and love… that's what life on this earth is all about. I pray that everyone can feel this same joy in their life. I didn't always have this, but I'm so thankful that I now have it in my heart."

God opened a door through my friend, Lisa, and got me even more excited for what He has in store for Be Love Give Love. Not only is Lisa driving all over the USA with the Be Love Give Love logo on her truck, but she is also spreading the love and lighting up the world by passing out Be Love Give Love appreciation cards. Simply amazing!! And I had nothing to do with this blessing because Lisa and I never discussed this. It was all God moving in her heart, and she just asked my permission to help spread the message of Be Love Give Love. It was amazing to watch the unfolding of the Wildfire Vision of 2007.

Chapter 22

THINGS ARE CHANGING AGAIN

Virtual Schooling

The following school year, we still had the option to do virtual schooling, which was great, because I knew Shia would not be able to handle attending the previous location. This time things would be very different. Ms. Hatcher got a well-deserved promotion and was no longer going to be his teacher for the 20-21 school year. It was hard to let her go because she had loved Shia like he was her very own.

I was still Shia's teacher at home, but I was reporting all his progress to his new teacher at school. Little by little, I took on more and more control of Shia's schooling in what to teach and how to teach it.

God began to speak to us about pulling Shia completely from the school system. Fortunately, God had faithfully built my confidence, so I surrendered and embraced what we were going through. I felt completely confident that I could be Shia's teacher. It always brought me so much joy to see Shia progressing beautifully and being happy, peaceful, and thriving in our home.

October 2020: Echocardiogram Appointment

The day came for what I was hoping to be my last echocardiogram. I was incredibly peaceful, steady, and stable... not swayed at all. The palpitations had lifted, and I was feeling great. I was hopeful that this long journey of persevering was about to come to an end, yet I trusted God with whatever results they gave me. Then I got the call with the results.

My cardiologist said, "All is clear, and you are released from all cardiac care." I cried happy tears and just sat there incredibly grateful and recalled all that God had brought me through and taught me. It was worth it all, and I would do it all over again to have the strength and wisdom I have now. Though it wasn't always easy, He never left me as I courageously stepped into this journey. He was there the entire time walking hand in hand with me. As I daily sought after Him, He faithfully encouraged, comforted and strengthened me as He gave me the endurance to walk the journey, despite everything else that I was going through. I am overwhelmed by His love for me.

Early 2021: Tim Deploys Again

This deployment was different in that Tim sat me down, and said he needed to ask me some questions. He then told me I needed to fill out some paperwork. In past deployments, he had never done this before leaving, so I thought it was a new Army requirement and didn't think too much about it.

Tim proceeded to ask me several questions: "If something happened to me while I was deployed, would you want someone to be with you when they told you?" "Do you want to contact the family to inform them of what happened, or do you want the Army to contact them?" He asked several other questions that I can't exactly remember, but all questions regarded what I would want done should Tim die while deployed.

I remained unshaken by these questions and was unwavering and firm in my faith. God had done an amazing work in my heart. He had purified me of those things that had previously kept me from living in freedom and having a deep trust in God.

At the beginning of Tim's deployment, we were due for our yearly termite inspection. A very nice gentleman did the inspection on the inside and outside of our home and then came inside. After making small talk, he asked if we were military, because they offered a military discount. Then with deep sympathy in his eyes, he softly asked if I was a widow. I was completely thrown off by his question, and my facial expression must have shown my surprise. Though I told him I wasn't a widow, I could tell he did not believe me.

When Tim has long deployments like that one, and because of the nature of his job, he wears a lot of civilian clothing, and his side of the closet is almost completely empty. At this time, I had moved a lot of Shia's things into our closet, because Shia was going through a phase of wanting to sleep close to me. And because his daddy was away, I freely allowed him that form of comfort. That might have been why the man assumed I was a widow.

Never, had I been asked if I was a widow, so with all the questions that Tim asked me before leaving, I was feeling intense waves of uncertainty crashing over me. I knew I had to stand against all the noise, the thoughts of *what-if,* and the sadness that tried to overtake me. It was yet another opportunity for a spiritual workout and to put into practice my training to trust God.

God reminded me of some things that He had taught me over the years. He said, "Remember, you are in a battle. Put up that shield of faith the moment you feel, sense, and see those fiery darts...those intense thoughts that try to attack your mind, and stand strong in Me. Also, remember just because you feel, sense, and see them doesn't mean that they have pierced you. They only pierce you when you sit with the emotion of the attack and stop fighting in the battle. Go into battle with My strength and you will not be moved. You will not be shaken."

The intense thoughts happened frequently during this deployment, but as I pressed into God and held up my shield of faith, I was able to stand steady and stable in my belief that God had this. I am happy to say that the enemy did not defeat me, and I came out of Tim's deployment stronger and with deeper roots in God.

Chapter 23

GOD'S DEEP REVELATIONS

Spring 2021: The Dream Changed

The dream I had been having over the years had shown me sitting on the bench instead of playing in the basketball game. When I woke up, I was so excited, that after eight years, the dream had finally changed. However, it still involved my senior year basketball coach and team. This time, I was eagerly sitting on the bench, watching the game, ready to play, and saying, "Put me in coach." But this time, my coach looked at me, and I knew it was almost time.

At half time, we were in the locker room at my high school, and I went to open my locker to get my shoes. For some reason, I was not wearing my basketball shoes, and I had forgotten the combination to the lock. My coach cut off the lock, opened my locker, and handed me my shoes. But the shoes were different.

The shoes were purple and gold, which were not our school colors. I put them on, and the dream shifted to me playing, but I was awful. I was stumbling all over the court, and I couldn't make a shot. To say I was a bit rusty is an understatement. Then the dream shifted to the opposing team player who was attacking me. She was trying to break my arm, and then I awakened from the dream.

I was left a bit disturbed after this dream, and I remember praying and asking God what it meant. Why was I back in the game but not playing at all well, and why was the other team trying to take me out? At that time, I didn't receive much revelation.

The Dream Changed Again

Several weeks later, the dream changed again. This time, I was playing very well and making shot after shot after shot. The crowd was cheering, and then suddenly, the dream shifted, and the players changed. I didn't recognize who they were. The team was huddled, and I was in the middle. I was the coach, coaching them, and then I woke up. I was super pumped that the dream had changed, and this time I was playing well.

Deeper Revelation of the Dreams

Sometime later, God was giving me deeper revelations regarding these dreams. I was, in fact, removed from "the game of life," not using my gifts and talents that God had given me, and sitting on the bench of life for a short time. This wasn't to punish me but to prune me, refine me, and purify me so I could be a better teacher and coach for others. My journey is proof that God is working it all together for good.

God also revealed that the very different shoes in the dream represented the shoes of peace in the armor of God (Ephesians 6:15). The shoes of peace give us a firm foundation, so we can stand firm, steady, and stable in the trials of life.

God then revealed why I was stumbling around on the court, unable to play well. During the last several years, I had been trying to find my footing in life, as He was tending to the deeper matters of my heart. He was in the process of helping me build an even firmer foundation, so that I could walk in peace through life's trials.

The meaning of the opposing team that tried to take me out, was like the fluid around my heart that tried to end my life. Despite the enemy's efforts, God miraculously sustained, protected, and preserved me.

I know that I have not fully arrived, and indeed there is more growth to occur as I continue my journey. Nevertheless, God revealed in this last dream that I was ready to coach people in how to put on the shoes of peace, so they too can walk in peace and be steady and stable when trials come their way.

Healing People

Before I wrote *Living Still*, I remember crying out to God and saying, "I want to pray for people and see them healed." I desperately wanted to be able to put my hands on people and see them get healed and have their pain taken away. Being the sensitive person that I am, I feel people's pain deeply. I wanted to be used by God to set people free from anything and everything that was taking their peace. I remember going to my husband and sharing with him my deep desire to bring healing to people. He said, "Maybe you aren't supposed to heal that way. Maybe you are supposed to help bring peace of mind to people." That hit my heart deeply in a beautiful way. I knew that was from God. It made perfect sense and makes even more sense now.

Take Your Best Shot

I was diagnosed with extreme panic disorder and eventually hit rock bottom in 2002 at the age of 24. It is truly remarkable that I am now in a place where my walk with God is so firmly rooted and planted in Him, that I can say to Satan..."Take your best shot, because I will not be moved."

There was a time, when the very thought of saying something that bold would have caused me so much fear. But now, I can say it and not tremble in fear, because I know God is with me! He has faithfully been with me, providing everything I need, throughout my entire journey, and I know beyond a shadow of a doubt, that He will continue to be with me.

I am no one special. God doesn't love me more than He loves you. This life of peace and freedom that I live, isn't available for only a select few. It is obtainable to anyone willing to do exactly what I did, and that is to choose to "fully" surrender your heart to God. That requires trusting Him deeply and allowing Him to deal with the matters of your heart that keep you from walking in peace and freedom and from being able to be love and give love to the world around you.

I understand your trials may be much different and more intense than my own have been. Please know that no matter the trials you are facing or the trials that may come your way, God will walk hand and hand with you on this journey. I promise that as you trust Him and keep your heart fully surrendered to Him, He will provide everything you need to get you to the other side, just as He faithfully did and continues to do for me.

Tim's rapid deployment left us unsure when he would return home. But once again, God's unending faithfulness brought him home to us in Spring of 2022. So, keep pressing into God. Keep persevering in Him. Don't give up. Keep moving forward, walking with Him. If you do, then just like I have done, you will stand in awe as you look back, and say, "It has all been worth it."

Chapter 24

INVITATION TO SHIA'S WORLD

Come Into My World

If Shia could talk and express his thoughts and feelings, I believe that from what I have watched over the years, he would say something like the following:

"Come into my world, and I will help you let go of the things that cause you to lose your peace. Just ask my daddy. Your world is too chaotic for me. Too much noise. Too much hurry. Too busy. Too loud. The energy of the people in your world is just too intense for me. Too much anger. Too much fear. Too much worry. Too much stress. Too much negativity.

In my world, life is simple, peaceful, and calm. I laugh often. I listen to music. I walk barefoot outside all the time. I sit in silence often. I enjoy the sunshine and all that nature has to offer. I spend more time outside than inside. I enjoy the simple things. I am content. I am joyful. I am peaceful. I am still. But...the moment I step into your world, everything changes. I feel the intensity of it all and it overwhelms me. I can't handle it, and if you are honest with yourself, you can't handle it either.

So, I invite you to take time to disconnect from your world, as often as you can and step into my world...Shia's world. I bet, just like my daddy, you will find it is easy to let go of all the stresses and burdens of life and find peace, love, and joy again. Sit in Shia's world long enough, and you will discover a longing for something you cannot find in the noise of your world.... a deeper sense of peace...a deeper connection with God."

A LETTER
FROM COACH ABBY

O h, to have the peace and tranquility of Shia's world, where
life is simple, peaceful, and calm. As a woman, wife, and
mother, who has learned the joy of being still in the Presence of
God, you too can find that peace and calm. My hope is that you
were so touched by my journey that it opened your eyes to the
realness of God's love for you and caused an awakening deep
within you…a yearning…a hunger…a deep desire to experience
more of His light and love in your own heart.

I believe that a great revival is coming and that the wildfire
vision that was spoken over me in 2007 will take place. But you
will never see revival and a mighty move of God unless you deal
with the matters of your own heart. That can only begin when you
allow God's light to expose the hidden things that cause darkness
within your heart. Only then can His love flow powerfully in and
through you to impact you and the world around you. That is Be
Love Give Love. That is where the wildfire begins…in you…in
your heart.

Remember Jesus' words when He spoke the parable of the soil
(heart). He said that if you don't understand this parable, how will

you understand *any* of the parables. Is this why we aren't seeing a mighty move of God? Think of how the world is today. What is flowing out of the hearts of people? Out of the overflow of the heart the mouth speaks. Are hearts lukewarm or perhaps they have grown cold and far from God? Where is the fire of God's love in hearts today?

I ask you to take a serious inventory of what is flowing from you...especially if you claim to be a follower of Jesus. This is not to condemn you but to awaken you. The world will know you are on fire for God by the overflow from your heart. And the fruits of the spirit are what should be flowing from you to others...love, joy, peace, patience, kindness, goodness, faithfulness, gentleness, and self-control.

God is using my precious son, Shia, to inspire you to go to that place of stillness to be in God's Presence. Follow Shia's example by choosing to take time to be still in God's Presence as often as you can. Step away from the chaos of the world, turn off your electronics, and take off your shoes to feel the grass between your toes. Connect with nature and enjoy the silence. It is in the still, quiet place that God's light exposes the darkness that is within your heart. And it is that darkness that prevents you from living a life of freedom and peace that you truly desire. It was in that very place of darkness, 20 years ago, that I hit rock bottom. But then God began to expose the darkness within my own heart and started a deep work within me.

The freedom that comes from living the posture of a surrendered heart is so incredibly worth it all. So, if you want to walk in God's freedom and power like I do, you must let go and let God deal with the matters of your heart.

I encourage you to surrender your heart fully to God and allow Him total access to every part of your heart. "Lord, I surrender my heart to You. Reveal those hidden things that have brought darkness into my heart and life. Direct and guide me each day. In Jesus' name. Amen."

Trust Him, as your Master Gardener. Let His love and light extinguish all the darkness, so revival can begin...within you...within us collectively...within the world.

Be Love Give Love

#belovegivelove #spreadthelove #lightuptheworld

DID GOD SPEAK TO YOUR HEART IN A SPECIAL WAY WHILE READING THIS BOOK?

I would love to hear from you.

Come share your thoughts with me at:
Facebook @beloveandgivelove
Instagram @belovegivelove

I invite you to visit the Be Love Give Love website and learn more about me and the products and services that I offer. You can listen to my podcast, shop the Be Love Give Love product line, and book speaking engagements.

www.belovegivelove.com

If you want to build a firm foundation for greater peace and stability in your life, then I encourage you to purchase my first book, *Living Still~Walking in Peace in the Midst of Life.*

This book gives the necessary tools and inspiration for you to begin working on the deeper matters of your heart that keep you from truly walking in peace during life's trials and radiating the love and light of God.

Made in the USA
Columbia, SC
02 October 2022